Notes on the Heart

Notes on the Heart

Affective Issues in the Writing Classroom

Susan H. McLeod

Southern Illinois University Press
Carbondale and Edwardsville

A portion of chapter 1 has been previously published as "The Affective
Domain and the Writing Process: Working Definitions," *Journal of Advanced
Composition* 11 (1991): 95–105. Reprinted with permission. A portion of
chapter 6 has been previously published as "Pygmalion or Golem? Teacher
Affect and Efficacy," *College Composition and Communication* 46.3 (1995):
369–84. Copyright 1995 by the National Council of Teachers of English.
Reprinted with permission.

Library of Congress Cataloging-in-Publication Data

McLeod, Susan H.
    Notes on the heart : affective issues in the writing classroom /
Susan H. McLeod.
        p.   cm.
    Includes bibliographical references and index.
    1. English language—Rhetoric—Study and teaching—Psychological
aspects. 2. Authorship—Psychological aspects. 3. Teacher-student
relationships. 4. Learning, Psychology of. 5. Motivation
(Psychology) 6. Affective education. 7. Authors—Psychology.
8. Emotions. I. Title.
PE1404.M394   1997
808'.042'07—dc20   96-17771
ISBN 0-8093-1738-9 (cloth : alk. paper)   CIP
ISBN 0-8093-2106-8 (alk. paper)

The paper used in this publication meets the minimum requirements of
American National Standard for Information Sciences—Permanence of
Paper for Printed Library Materials, ANSI Z39.48-1984. ∞

This book is dedicated to Sue Hallett, without whom it would never have been rewritten, and to my family, whose support was, as always, generous and unfailing.

Thus, great with child to speak, and helpless in my throes,
Biting my truant pen, beating myself for spite:
"Fool," said my Muse to me, "look in thy heart, and write!"

—Sir Philip Sidney, *Astrophel and Stella*

Contents

Preface

A word about the collaboration of Susans that has led to this book. The idea for the book and the eventual first draft came from Susan McLeod. Appropriately enough, the book grew out of an affective experience: a vague feeling of dissatisfaction with the explanatory power of both cognitive and social constructionist theories of the composing process. Let me, the first Susan, hasten to say that I have found both these approaches to researching and teaching composition most helpful, as readers will discover throughout this book; both provide useful ways of conceptualizing issues and of putting theory into practice in the classroom. I have found Linda Flower's newest book, *The Construction of Negotiated Meaning: A Social Cognitive Theory of Writing* (Carbondale: Southern Illinois UP, 1994) to be especially insightful.

But various encounters, familiar to all teachers of composition, told me I needed to know more about matters of the heart. There was Alice, the student who remained satisfied with her first drafts and didn't revise, even though her editing group (and her teacher) told her rather insistently that her work needed revision. Then there was Leontina, the student who usually wrote well but produced a very disjointed paper on a topic she obviously cared deeply about. There was Ira, the student who told me that he had never been good at English, his voice and manner suggesting that it was hopeless to try; he was defeated before he started, putting little effort into the assignments because he knew he would fail. Most frustrating to me were the students (more numerous than I liked to admit) who seemed to care more about grades than about improving their writing. How could I deal—and help students deal in productive ways—with what seemed to be affective rather than social/cognitive issues?

So I researched and wrote. The first draft of the book was what Ernest Boyer would call the "scholarship of integration." It was a review of the research on affect, drawing primarily from psychology, sociology, and anthropology, fascinating stuff. Still, the dissatisfaction lingered; the draft seemed too—well, cerebral, an intellectual discussion of affect. Reviewers of the manuscript made suggestions, the most helpful of which was to provide more situatedness, more application to day-to-day classroom interactions. For one semester, I conducted a modest teacher-research project in my own English 101 class, discussing affective issues with students and collecting data. I then found a new administrative position thrust upon me, making a regular 101 teaching assignment difficult.

Thus began the collaboration with Sue Hallett, Susan #2, an instructor in Washington State University's composition program. Sue, a former medical social worker and special education teacher, is one of the most effective teachers in the writing program, at least from her students' point of view. In their evaluations, they praise her sympathy and understanding of them as well as her efforts in pushing them to do their best. The next semester, I observed Sue's class and took notes, interviewed students, read copies of their papers, and met with Sue to discuss what I saw in her class. The following semester, Susan Parker (Susan #3) became part of our collaborative effort. This third Susan, a new graduate student in our program, was observing Sue Hallett's class as part of her T.A. training and was also running a tutorial connected to that class.[1] Thus she was uniquely positioned to help us understand more fully what we saw, or what we thought we saw, in the classroom interactions that semester. Susan #2 and #3 kept teaching journals, I continued to r ead student papers and conduct interviews, and the three of us met weekly to discuss what was going on in Sue's classes and how certain events and student behaviors were illuminated by the theories set forth in this book.

What emerged from this study for us was a fuller understanding of affect in the classroom. In the account that follows, we have conflated the year and a half of our study into one semester in order to provide a narrative for the book. The class is a composite drawn from seven classrooms over three semesters; the students are real enough (we have changed only their names and a few identifying features), but they were not all in the same class. The narrative of the semester is not an ethnography—rather it is a story that provides illustrations of theory being played out in a particular context. We hope that by presenting a classroom context with illustrative vignettes, the research on affect will be more accessible for teachers like ourselves who want to understand our students better so that we can better help them with their writing.

Philosophers have had much to say about the affective domain, and we recommend their work to those interested in such musings. (See, for example, Heidegger, Kierkegaard, Langer, Sartre. A useful summary of such approaches is provided by Calhoun and Solomon.) We have relied for the most part, however, on research from the social sciences; this reliance is not because philosophy has nothing to teach us, but because we, the writers, tend to be more pragmatic than philosophical. Our discussions of pedagogy, while they are meant to be of practical value, are intended to be suggestive rather than prescriptive. In fact, many writing teachers are already using some of the suggested techniques and approaches but perhaps had not thought of them in light of affective phenomena. We hope the discussion will help such teachers see their practice in a new way. Readers will note that there is a common thread through these discussions of pedagogy—the need for students and teachers to become aware of theory, to know themselves more fully, to examine their own affective as well as cognitive processes in order to understand (and therefore regulate or even change) these processes.

Finally, a word about how we, the Susans, refer to ourselves in the chapters that follow. While the work is collaborative, we found it awkward to try to refer to ourselves as "we," especially after deciding to combine the various classrooms into one. The teacherly "I" of this book is therefore a conflation of the first two Susans, McLeod and Hallett, enriched with insights we gained from our third Susan, the participant-observer and helpful editor.

The debts for this project are many. Washington State University provided generous research support in the form of a summer research grant and a yearlong sabbatical for Susan McLeod. Many colleagues read and commented on drafts of the manuscript, giving their ideas and helping us clarify our own; we are especially grateful to Doug McLeod, Elenore Long, Joseph Petraglia, Shirley Rose, Sherry Little, Lucille Parkinson McCarthy, Susan Wyche, Lori Weist, Marie Glenn, and Rachel Halverson for their perceptive comments and suggestions. We are also indebted to the anonymous reviewers for Southern Illinois University Press. Finally, our family members supported us, as they always do, with their encouragement and understanding. To all, but especially the latter, we owe much gratitude.

Notes on the Heart

❦ 1 ❦

Beginnings
Learning the Names

The emotions are excellent examples of the fictional
causes to which we commonly attribute behavior.
—B. F. Skinner, *Science and Human Behavior*

The first day of class. It is the end of August, still very
warm in the Pacific Northwest. Here on our rural, residen-
tial campus, most freshmen are really fresh—eighteen years
old, away from home for the first time, excited, scared. I'm a
little excited myself. The task ahead of me—beginning again,
introducing myself in front of 25 pairs of eyes—always results in some measure of performance anxiety. (How many
teachers have the same dream I do the night before classes
start? I arrive at the class a few minutes late to discover that
I have the wrong room, or the wrong book, or no handouts,
or no clothes.) When I walk into the room, I pick up a little
of the electricity in the air; it crackles from the students to
me and back again. The choir directors of my youth used to
say we should be keyed up rather than nervous, so as to perform at peak. Channel that energy, they would say—make
your butterflies fly in formation. I smile at a student, who
responds shyly with her own smile. I begin to feel calmer.

My job on this first day is twofold: to start to learn who
these writers are and—in spite of all the necessary official
handouts listing requirements and admonishing them about
plagiarism and responsible library use—to also reassure them

about the nature of the class, to create a positive and supportive atmosphere. Whatever I say, my subtext is always
this: "It's OK, you can do this. You are all writers, and I am
here to help you understand and use the strengths you already have." I begin by introducing myself, mentioning that
I have kids their age—a fact that I hope makes me seem less
threatening, more approachable. I want students to feel safe
enough to take risks with their writing. I call roll, and we do
an icebreaker in which they interview and then introduce a
class member to the rest of us. We all begin to learn the names.

Melanie. She's the older woman in the back, her worn
polyester blouse and slacks a contrast to all the casually ex-
pensive junior sportswear around her. The person introducing her mentions that Melanie also has college-age kids; I
find out later that she is a high school dropout who recently
passed the GED exam without studying. Heather. Her T-
shirt proclaims her a member of Youth for Christ; she has
the fresh-faced look of rural America. Tom and Chad. They
are wearing identical fraternity polos and sit staring off into
space with studied disinterest; even though I had asked
people to interview someone they didn't know, they interview each other, introducing themselves in tandem as "totally cool." Alberto. A transplant from southern California,
he volunteers proudly that he attended a well-known paro-
chial prep school on a scholarship for Chicano students.
Leontina. She is so soft-spoken we can hardly hear her; she
wears a baseball cap with an X on the front over beautifully
elaborate cornrows. Alice. She says earnestly and publicly
that she is very anxious to add my class (I find out later it is
so that she can take the course with her friend Jane, who sits
next to her). Ed. His large, muscular frame makes him look
much older than the average lanky freshman; we find out
that he has just been discharged from the military and is cel-
ebrating by growing a beard. An Mei. A native of Hong
Kong, she has come here to study pharmacy. All her friends
placed in the ESL sections, and she expresses some surprise
at being in a "real" composition class. Ira. His baby face and

halo of blonde hair make him look much younger than his classmates; we find out that he lives with his grandmother and that he has "never been good at English." Rod. Just off the family dairy farm, he is here on an academic scholarship. He has a passion for fly-fishing. Will. He looks a bit disheveled; we discover that he reads a lot of Hemingway and wants to be a writer. Jaymie. She wears a lot of makeup and a shirt identifying her with a sorority known for its memorable parties. She demonstrates a quick wit, immediately challenging any stereotype we might hold about sorority women.

I move on to a discussion of the general outline for the semester ahead. Freshman composition at this institution requires academic writing assignments based on multicultural readings. The writing tasks are demanding intellectually—students are often asked to read and think about emotional, value-laden issues and then write in the discourse of the academy, that is, in an analytical, objective fashion. The course also involves portfolio assessment, based on the system established by Elbow and Belanoff at SUNY Stony Brook, whereby another teacher will read my students' papers and decide on whether or not they will pass the course. Those of us in this room are a diverse lot; I know that the provocative texts we read will evoke complex affective reactions from the students as well as for me, and that the task of preparing a portfolio for an unknown reader will arouse anxiety among many. I wonder what the next few months hold for us all. The first writing assignment has to do with encountering the "other": a personal narrative and analysis of a moment of cultural encounter, a fitting metaphor for the experience we are initiating together today. I assign the readings: Edward Hall's "Anthropology of Manners," Simone de Beauvoir's "Woman as Other," Es'kia Mphahlele's short story "The Master of Doornvlei," Paul Laurence Dunbar's poem "We Wear the Mask."[1]

I ask them to do a freewrite on an encounter they have had with someone different, or with different manners or customs. Toward the end of the class period, Ira tells me in a rather querulous tone that I have assigned too much to read. Feeling slightly irritated, I promise to help explain things and ask him to stay for a minute after class, but he strolls out with Tom and Chad. My irritation turns to annoyance; I don't like his attitude, and it's only the first day. Two other students linger to voice their anxieties about the class. Rod tells me that he needs to maintain a 3.0 GPA to retain his scholarship, seeming concerned already that he won't be able to make the grade. I assure him that while I can't predict or promise grades, if he works hard I will work with him just as hard. An Mei is worried—did she do the in-class assignment correctly? I tell her that all freewrites are "correct" and talk a bit more about the purpose of the exercise. She seems satisfied (but she will continue to check with me about her progress every day after class for the next few weeks). I leave the classroom, mentally reviewing names and faces for next time.

I work at learning student names quickly so that I can begin to mentally organize helpful information as I learn more about each of them as writers. Through the coming semester we will hit various affective bumps together. The chapters of this book will discuss our semester, first describing classroom encounters familiar to teachers of composition and then presenting the research that has helped me and I hope will help other teachers understand the nature of these encounters. In order to discuss the affective domain precisely, however, we need more naming, more introductions, this time to the terms that will be used in this book. But first, some background about why writing teachers need to think about affective issues and why it is so difficult for us to do so.

Coming to Terms with Affect

It should not be difficult for writing teachers and researchers to discuss affect (that is, the noncognitive aspects of human behavior, especially the emotions). We are accustomed to viewing humans as both thinking and feeling individuals; the dichotomy of head and heart is so ingrained in Western thought that it seems natural to think of one when thinking of the other. Yet it has always been difficult to discuss affective issues in a systematic way, primarily because of the Western cultural bias against affect as a serious topic of academic interest.

As one psychologist points out, the Western attitude toward emotion is inherited from the Greeks, who saw cognition and affect as opposed to one another. Cognition was rational, affect was irrational (Lazarus 252); rational was good, irrational usually was not. Our culture views emotion as getting in the way of reason, interfering with proper (reasonable) action. "Cognition is sober inspection; it is the scientist's calm apprehension of fact after fact in his relentless pursuit of Truth. Emotion, on the other hand, is commotion—an unruly inner turbulence fatal to such pursuit but finding its own constructive outlets in aesthetic experience and moral or religious commitment" (Scheffler 347). The words and phrases we use to describe emotional states (lovesick, hotheaded, grief-stricken) indicate that our culture sees affect as something that happens to us, rather like a viral invasion, an affliction for which we are not responsible and cannot control. The affective realm has also long been identified in Western culture with the feminine, weak side of human nature. In the famous scene where Melville's Captain Vere announces his decision to hang Billy Budd, for example, he has this to say:

> [T]he exceptional in the matter moves the hearts within
> you. Even so too is mine moved. But let not warm hearts
> betray heads that should be cool. Ashore in a criminal case,
> will an upright judge allow himself off the bench to be
> waylaid by some tender kinswoman of the accused seeking
> to touch him with her tender plea? Well the heart here,

sometimes the feminine in man, is as that piteous woman,
and hard though it be, she must here be ruled out. (111)

When the study of human behavior became system-
atized in the field we now call psychology, scientists took
much the same view as Captain Vere. Freud, although attributing a good deal of behavior to the power of passion,
viewed emotions as potentially harmful forces to be acknowledged and properly tamed. As behavioral psychology became more dominant in the discipline, affect was discounted
as trivial. One behaviorist argued that the concept of emotion was useless, since the features of behavior that emotion
supposedly explained were features of all behavior (Duffy
292). Others rejected emotion as a concept suitable for study
because it was not substantive enough (Brown and Farber
466), that is, it was "fictional" (according to Skinner) in terms
of explaining behavior scientifically. More recently, the cognitive perspective has gained ascendancy in psychology;
cognitivists view humans as problem-solvers whose minds
operate rather like computers in their processing, storing,
and retrieving of information. But since computers do not
feel, it was at first difficult for those who use an information-
processing model of the mind to decide where affect should
go in that model. It was easiest to ignore the emotions, or to
view affect simply as "a regrettable flaw in an otherwise perfect cognitive machine" (Scherer 293).

But of course every time we walk into a classroom on
the first day, we are newly aware of the affective realm. We
cannot ignore it, nor should we consider it in isolation from
the cognitive domain as we think about the psychology of
writing. As Vygotsky said, the separation of affect from cognition

is a major weakness of traditional psychology, since it
makes the thought process appear as an autonomous flow

of "thoughts thinking themselves," segregated from the fullness of life, from the personal needs and interests, the inclinations and impulses, of the thinker. Such segregated thought must be viewed either as a meaningless epiphenomenon incapable of changing anything in the life or conduct of a person or else as some kind of primeval force exerting an influence on personal life in an inexplicable, mysterious way. The door is closed on the issue of the causation and origin of our thoughts, since deterministic analysis would require clarification of the motive forces that direct thought into this or that channel. By the same token, the old approach precludes any fruitful study of the reverse process, the influence of thought on affect and volition. (10)

We need to come to terms with affect, viewing the affect/ cognition split not as a dichotomy but as a dialectic.

In order to discuss affective issues carefully, we need a shared vocabulary with which to discuss affect—we need to learn the names for the affective states we encounter, both in ourselves and in our students. Because of the personal, subjective nature of the domain, the noncognitive aspects of human activity have been notoriously difficult for the scientific community to define (see Verplanck); aside from general agreement that there is a domain we may label "affective," there is not much agreement on how to describe it further. As one psychologist observes, the word "affect" has been used by psychologists to include a wide range of concepts and phenomena, including feelings, emotions, moods, motivation, and certain drives and instincts. "Theorists and researchers have approached affect in numerous ways, often using idiosyncratic, contradictory or mutually exclusive conceptualizations and operational definitions that have resulted in confusing and limited progress in our understanding of affect or any . . . related or synonymous constructs" (Corsini 32). Indeed, at the 1981 Carnegie Symposium on Cognition, the subject of which was "Affect and Cognition," Herbert Simon, a founder of the field we now call cognitive science, called attention to the difficulty of discussing a concept that seemed to have a number of different meanings for those presenting papers at the meeting:

> I have some impression, in moving from one paper to the next, that we are indeed the traditional blind men, now touching one part of the elephant, now another. Affect is a word of everyday language that is subject to the imprecision of all such words—perhaps to more imprecision than most. Its various meanings are connected—that's how they arose in the first place—but not synonymous. (334)

Here I will introduce more names, this time names for affective states, in an attempt to clarify the meanings of various terms most commonly used by psychologists to describe affective phenomena. These names, along with the names of students, will recur throughout the book as we progress through a semester in a composition class. After the umbrella term "affect," the terms defined below move along a continuum of sorts from those that have the least cognitive involvement (emotion, feeling, mood) to those that have the most (motivation, intuition).[2] I have kept as much as possible the ordinary use of these terms, intending not to give new stipulative definitions of familiar terms but to suggest more precise, focused meanings for them. It should be understood that the concepts being defined are in fact hypothetical constructs—none of us has seen an emotion or an attitude, only responses that lead us to believe that such things exist. The definitions are intended to be descriptive so that their precise meaning as they are used in subsequent chapters will be clear. At various points I will also mention areas where we need to know more about the relationship of affect and writing, for those who might wish to explore those areas themselves.

Affect

The word "affect" embraces a wide variety of constructs and processes that do not fit neatly under the heading of "cognition." Besides the varied use by psychologists noted above, educators have employed the term to describe attitudes, beliefs, tastes, appreciations, and preferences. The best-known use of the term in this broad sense is the handbook by Krathwohl, Bloom, and Masia, *Taxonomy of Educational Objectives: The Affective Domain*. I am guided by Simon (335) and by Clore, Ortony, and Foss to suggest that we use "affect" as a generic term to describe such phenomena as emotions, attitudes, beliefs, moods, and conation (motivation); I also include one phenomenon not listed by these psychologists, intuition. Affect is therefore not a synonym for emotion; an emotion is an affective state, but not all affective states are emotions.

It is important to note that the cognition/affect dialectic should not be equated with rationality/ irrationality, as it often is in common usage. "Cognition" as it is used by most psychologists refers to the processing of information and invoking of knowledge, both conscious and unconscious, deliberate and automatic; it does not mean only rational, thought-like processes (Lazarus 252–53). An affective state, on the other hand, can be a very rational (in the sense of appropriate and reasonable) response to a situation. It should also be noted that the affective phenomena described below all have some cognitive component; as Piaget noted, "[A]t no level, at no state, even in the adult, can we find a behavior or a state that is purely cognitive without affect nor a purely affective state without a cognitive element involved" (qtd. in Derry and Murphy 13).

Emotion

William James posed the scientific question "What is

an emotion?" in 1884, but there is still little agreement in the psychological community about the answer. Scientists have tried to identify and group various emotions, with contradictory results. Some researchers (Tomkins; Izard; Plutchik) subscribe to a "palette" theory of fundamental emotions that can be blended, rather like primary colors, to make up secondary emotions (contempt, for example, is made up of two primary emotions, surprise and disgust). Others have discredited such a theory (G. Mandler, *Mind* 34–37; Averill, "Constructivist" 326–29), pointing out that even those who believe in primary emotions cannot agree what those fundamental emotions are and that there is evidence of cultural variation among emotional systems that would contradict the idea of universal fundamental emotions (Harré 10–12). Another classification system, that of Ortony, Clore, and Collins, begins with the cognitive construals that determine emotional states. These researchers first define three broad classes of emotions that result from focusing on three aspects of the world: events and their consequences, agents and their actions, and objects. They then describe what they refer to as "emotion types" (15), discussing the eliciting conditions and influencing variables of emotions (for example, one can be pleased or displeased about the consequences of an event, approve or disapprove of the actions of an agent, like or dislike an object). For example, Ortony and his associates discuss anxiety as one of the "fear emotions"—that is, a reaction to the prospect of an undesirable event or outcome.

But whatever their particular stance on the number of and names for emotions, cognitive psychologists generally agree that emotions consist of a bodily activation (arousal of the autonomic nervous system involving a visceral reaction—increased heartbeat, a knot in the stomach, a heightened awareness of external stimuli) and a cognitive evaluation of that activation (see Kleinginna and Kleinginna, "Emotion Definitions"). Most also agree that these evaluations are valenced (for example, labeled as negative or positive) and that they range in intensity (some, like anger, are "hot"; some, like hope, less so). There is growing interest in affect and the writing process, as evidenced by the work of such scholars as Lynn Bloom, Brand, Fleckenstein, Flower (*Construction*), Larson, McLeod, and Selfe.

The most studied emotion in writing research is anxiety, an affective state characterized by tension (both physical and mental), worry, and feelings of uneasiness about an undesirable event or outcome (see Ortony, Clore, and Collins 109–13). A useful distinction can be made between two forms of this affective phenomenon—trait anxiety and state anxiety (Spielberger). Trait anxiety is for some persons a habitual response to the vicissitudes of life; such persons are mildly anxious or fearful under all circumstances (like the student who writes well but frets over every assignment). State anxiety, on the other hand, is a more intense reaction to a particular circumstance. There are many studies of writing anxiety (see Smith; Rose, *Writer's Block*). However, these studies sometimes fail to differentiate between the two forms of anxiety, or between different forms of the phenomenon in the same students. Students who are anxious about writing for a grade are sometimes quite comfortable with writing for self-expression or writing letters (L. Bloom, "Composing Processes"; Perl, "Unskilled," "A Look") and therefore should be labeled as "anxious" or "high apprehensives" only in certain writing situations. Many such studies have also neglected the relationship between writing anxiety and other state anxiety situations; test anxiety, for example, would seem to be related to writing anxiety (especially in timed writing situations; see I. Sarason).

Less intense and more lingering, global affective states (such as contentment or dissatisfaction) may be thought of as moods. There are a number of studies that suggest a relationship between moods and information storage and retrieval—between mood and memory, as well as mood and learning (Bower; Bower and Cohen; Bastick; Kuiken; Morris). In other words, there is evidence that affect can direct and influence cognitive activities; there is, however, little research on the connection between writers' moods and how those moods might facilitate or inhibit writing.

The term "feelings" is often used in ordinary parlance as synonymous to "emotions" and has been used in that sense by some who write about affect (McLeod, "Some Thoughts"; Stein and Levine). Such usage creates difficulties, however, since some feelings are emotions but others are not: one can feel hungry as well as angry. Since "feeling" usually refers to bodily sensation, it might be more accurate to use the noun "feelings" to refer to those sensations that are part of the affective experience—the sweaty palms, constricted breath, dry mouth, and other symptoms of arousal of the autonomic nervous system, as well as the more diffuse sensations of moods (for example, feelings of lassitude). The verb "to feel" would then describe the bodily sensations associated with an emotion or a mood. Feelings can be thought of as part of an emotional experience but not necessarily synonymous with that experience. Emotions will be discussed more fully in chapter 2; classroom encounters with Ed, Alice, Leontina, Tom, and Chad will help illuminate issues of emotion.

Motivation

While there is some question as to whether or not conative aspects of mental activity should be classified under affect or should be considered separately, it is clear that motivation has an affective component. Motivation (Alexander Bain called it "will") refers to the internal states that lead to "the instigation, persistence, energy, and direction of behavior" (Corsini 395), to setting goals and energizing goal-directed behavior characterized by "impulse, desire, volition, purposive striving" (English and English 104). Motivation can be physiological (thirst motivates me to find water) or psychological (anxiety about a deadline motivates me to finish my work; see Kleinginna and Kleinginna, "Motivation Definitions"). Researchers distinguish between two kinds of psychological motivation: extrinsic (in a classroom setting, getting good grades, pleasing the teacher, working toward a career goal) or intrinsic (wanting to achieve success or avoid failure). There is evidence to suggest that while extrinsic motivation is important in learning situations, intrinsic motivation and self-direction are in fact more powerful (Deci, *Intrinsic*; Nicholls). More recently, psychologists have looked at motivation in the context of achievement motivation; an interesting branch of this research is attribution theory, an area that examines what people perceive as the cause for certain outcomes (as, for example, success or failure at academic tasks; see Weiner, *Attributional Theory*). The theory of learned helplessness, where students who feel they have no control over their success or failure simply give up at the first sign of difficulty (Diener and Dweck), is also of interest to writing teachers. This and other motivational theories will be discussed further in chapter 3, where the experiences of Alice, An Mei, Will, and Ira will illuminate these theories.

Beliefs and Attitudes

Beliefs have been defined as our judgments of the credibility of a concept or idea, "non-observable theoretical entities postulated to account for certain observable relations in human behavior" (Colby 253–54). Milton Rokeach, perhaps the best-known researcher on the subject, defines beliefs as "inferences made by an observer about underlying states of expectancy"—beliefs can be inferred from all the things the believer says or does (*Beliefs* 2). Rokeach defines values as central beliefs about how one ought or ought not to behave, or about some state of existence that is worthwhile or not; values are abstract representations of positive or negative ideals of conduct or goals (124). Other researchers suggest that the value we place upon a task is a function of three components: the attainment value of the task, its intrinsic interest, and its utility value for our future goals (Eccles et al.); these values are culturally as well as individually determined. Beliefs about task value determine how people set achievement goals for themselves and are therefore an important part of the motivational process.

Although there are a number of general studies examining teacher beliefs about instruction (Nespor; Schoenfeld; Wehling and Charters), there has been little research on teacher and/or student beliefs about the nature and value of writing and the writing process since the 1984 study by Gere, Schuessler, and Abbott. Such research would seem promising, with important implications for preparing writing teachers at all levels. One recent study, for example, shows that 72 percent of the students in the total sample (247) believed that the most important purpose of writing is self-knowledge and self-expression. If a teacher believes the primary purpose of writing is persuasion, students and teacher will be working at cross-purposes (Palmquist and Young 161). Aside from the studies based on attitude questionnaires, research having to do with student beliefs about themselves as writers is also sparse (see Silva and Nichols). These beliefs are no doubt related to such psychological constructs as self-concept and attributions of success and failure as well as to the specific subject of writing. They would also seem to be related to cultural beliefs about writing and the societal value placed upon writing, issues that are of importance as we discuss theories of the social construction of knowledge in composition. And what about students' personal belief systems and how those interact with their writing? Writing teachers are all too familiar with the papers—often on religion but sometimes on other issues—that are impassioned sermons rather than reasoned arguments. How does a given student's belief system affect his or her ability to write about issues that either affirm or challenge that system?

Attitudes spring from beliefs. Social psychologist Gordon Allport, writing in 1935, defined attitude as "a mental or neural state of readiness, organized through experience, exerting a directive or dynamic influence upon the individual's response to all objects and situations with which it is related" ("Attitudes" 810). In other words, attitudes are psychological entities acquired over a period of time as a result of experience; these attitudes influence us to act in certain ways and to respond to the world in a relatively consistent fashion. An attitude is not a response but a readiness to respond in particular ways. Allport's definition is still the standard one, with some recent modifications (see Rajecki). Those who write about attitudes often assume three components, based on a model put forward by Rosenberg and Hovland in 1960; these components are affect, behavior, and cognition. An affective reaction is usually part of an attitude, acting as an evaluative element (labeling the object of the attitude good or bad, positive or negative). Behavior is the intentional element, indicating what we do as a result of our attitudes. We might view attitudes as similar to emotions but less intense and more stable over time.

Most attitude theories emphasize individualistic, subjective phenomena; these theories neglect, however, the social aspect of acquiring and expressing attitudes. Richard Eiser points out that while attitudes may be private, the expression of attitude is a social act, and that attitude should be studied as a social product as well as a subjective experience. Eiser defines the term as "the meaning of a person's expressive behavior" (5), arguing that the relationship between attitudes and behavior is not necessarily a causal one (as is often assumed) but a logical one, based on social as well as personal factors. This view of attitudes being socially as well as privately constructed phenomena fits with the social constructionist view of knowledge. It also suggests that if our students' negative attitudes toward writing are the result of social as well as individual factors, then we need to think about how to establish in the writing classroom collaborative activities aimed not only at cognitive but also at attitudinal changes brought about by the group process. Chapter 4 provides a fuller discussion of beliefs, values, and attitudes; encounters with Alberto, Heather, and Jaymie during the semester illustrate this discussion.

Intuition

This term is used by psychologists to describe both the knowledge and understanding that come through nonrational means and the process by which that knowledge comes (Harré and Lamb). Related concepts are insight, that moment of illumination and intuitive comprehension, and inspiration, that feeling of tension and excitement that accompanies an insightful experience. These concepts have been associated over the centuries with religious as well as artistic and scientific problem-solving experiences. For the present discussion, however, I assume that intuition is a way of knowing but that it does not necessarily lead to truth (or to Truth). Intuition is the subject of chapter 5, where Rod's experience illustrates the phenomenon.

A Theoretical Framework for Discussing Affect

Besides terminology, we need a theoretical framework to inform our discussion of affect. Which of the several perspectives from which researchers have begun to examine affect is the most useful to writing teachers?[3] Let us briefly examine some of the major strands of research in the field. First of all, it is clear that there are certain biological factors involved in affective experiences; one strand of research examines the biology and chemistry of emotion, looking at physiological and neuroendocrinological phenomena. The biological research on affect asks such questions as "What exactly is the 'gut' reaction we feel during emotional experiences? How and where is the reaction processed and regulated by the brain? How do various biological factors (such as body metabolism) affect emotion?" The questions are answered by looking at data gathered by testing bodily reactions in the laboratory, using such instruments as the EEG (see, for example, Pribram; Davidson) or analysis of metabolic functions (Whybrow).

Another way of looking at affect is psychoevolutionary, harking back to Darwin's theory of emotions as common to both animals and humans. This strand of research examines the adaptational responses of animals for clues to human behavior (see Plutchik); one branch of this research looks at animal communication, discussing such matters as whether this communication is affective or cognitive (see Marler). While this strand of research does not appear immediately applicable to the writing process, it is helpful in underlining for us the fact that emotions are physiological as well as psychological phenomena.

Other researchers examine developmental aspects of the affective domain, asking such questions as "How early can humans be said to have affective reactions? How do emotional systems develop and what influences their development?" These researchers look particularly at infants' emotional states (for example, Emde) and at the role of affect and social interaction, especially communication (Trevarthen). Some assume that cognition and emotion are generated by different systems and examine how one system influences the other as children develop (Case, Hayward, Lewis, and Hurst). Writing researchers discuss students' intellectual development; clearly we need also to attend to their affective development as well.

There are anthropological approaches to the study of affect, approaches that ask questions about the cultural variability of affective responses, the conceptualization and naming of emotions in different cultures, and the cultural factors that contribute to affect (see Levy). These researchers often concentrate on facial expressions and what they signify in different cultures (see Ekman). There is also a strand of research that relies on questionnaires as instruments to determine the subject's affective response, especially anxiety, in various circumstances.[4] As we attend more and more to cultural difference in our university classrooms, in the curriculum and in the diversity of our students, cultural differences having to do with affect will be important for teachers to understand.[5]

    While all these perspectives on affect provide interesting information, there are two perspectives on affect that are of particular interest to writing teachers and researchers: that of the cognitive psychologist and that of the social constructionist. The former category is a rather large umbrella to shelter a somewhat disparate group of researchers, all of whose theories can be characterized by one shared idea, first put forward by Schachter and Singer: that the emotional experience is made up of an arousal of the nervous system and a valenced (positive or negative) cognitive appraisal of the bodily signals.[6] The theory of George Mandler stands out as the most useful for those of us in composition studies, since it fits the well-known cognitive-process model proposed by Flower and Hayes. The idea of the social construction of knowledge is viewed with growing interest in composition; Rom Harré and his associates have worked out a theory that examines affect as part of a social system. The next chapter enlarges upon these two theories, examining how emotion and cognition intertwine in the writing process.

❦ 2 ❦

Emotion

[P]sychology has been the beneficiary and the
prisoner of our most fascinating proclivity—to
explain the world around us, to understand what
surrounds us, to make up stories . . . that explain and
make comprehensible the evidence of our senses. . . .
Over the centuries the men and women who made up
the most convincing stories were elevated to a special
position in the life of the mind; first they were the
prophets, then the philosophers, and finally, the
scientists.

—George Mandler, *Mind and Body*

Why Aren't Things Going Better?

It's the third week of class. By now my major goal for
the first segment of the semester has been accomplished: I
know all my students' names and they are beginning to know
one another, becoming a community of writers. I pass back
the freewrites they have done and ask them to trade papers
just to see what others have written; there is laughter and
good-natured praise expressed for the ideas of others. Still,
I am not entirely happy with how the class is going—the
students are a little too subdued, too passive. Perhaps part
of the problem is the room, in the bowels of one of the oldest
buildings on campus, where the lighting is poor and it's small
enough that students can't get into groups comfortably. I

call and ask the powers that assign rooms to move us, and we are put in the queue. The 9 A.M. hour may also be a problem; for college students, that is daybreak. I bring in a coffeepot on Wednesday and before we start open all the windows to get some fresh air. The students brighten a bit, and by the end of the hour they are more animated. I get the message that a room in a newer building is available and we move on Friday; the room is bigger, the chairs are more comfortable, the lighting is better—I begin to feel that the class atmosphere may improve.

A couple of encounters with students puzzle and intrigue me. One is in our first session in the computer lab, a facility in which we will meet regularly, once a week. Most students have at least some acquaintance with computers (some have their own), but logging on to the network was new to them all. Ed, the student just out of the army, was trying the same strategy over and over but failing to log on. When I went over to help, he was rigid with frustration. "I should be able to do this! I've been working on a computer for the last two years!" I discover he is using a strategy from his previous experience (involving logging on to a mainframe rather than on to a network), and we talk about how difficult it is to switch from one computer environment to another. I go over the instructions with him once more; he gets on to the network, relaxes, and starts to write. I wonder why he persisted in using the same log-on strategy again and again when he could see that it did not work the first time.

Another puzzling encounter is with Alice. The first paper is due soon; we have been discussing the readings, all of which have to do with what one might call cultural encounters. Now they are to describe and analyze an encounter they have had with the "other," with another culture or another way of doing things. Alice is having trouble—she says she finds the topic "boring." In a conference she tells me she has nothing to write about, that she had never encountered the "other." I discover she is from San Francisco; hasn't she found any differences between the city and our small college town that she could write about? Did one of the readings, Hall's "Anthropology of Manners," give her any ideas? Her response: "People here seem different—they seem friendlier." Fine, write about that. The resulting draft is a description of an incident in San Francisco where a man asked for directions and was ignored, and a paragraph on how much nicer people are in our little college town. There is no analysis of the incident. She does not seem interested in revising, even though her peer editing group and I have given her a number of suggestions as to how she might analyze the incident in light of the readings on the "other." Her friend Jane, with whom she always sits and on whom she seems to depend for help, also gives her some good suggestions; she smiles and nods agreeably, and doesn't revise.

Leontina is having difficulty getting her ideas down in a coherent fashion, even though she (unlike Alice) is obviously engaged in her topic. Her cultural encounter was a fairly ugly racial incident in her high school—a fight that grew out of a misunderstanding about where and with whom people sat at lunch. She was still very upset about the way it was handled by the white principal, feeling that he was unfair to her fellow African American students; her description of the incident is disjointed and hard to follow. I ask her to reread Orwell's "Shooting an Elephant" and then write in her reading journal about the cues he gives readers to show how the incident unfolded, thinking she might find his deft chronology a model. I worry about the students in her writing group, who seemed to me during the discussion of Orwell's piece to be fairly naive about cultural difference. Will they be able to help her, or will the paper make Leontina the "other" in their eyes, cutting off any useful discussion? I decide that I will change the groups in the class around and put her in one with two other students who have written about similar experiences (Alberto, whose topic is gang activity in southern California, and Ed, who was horrified by the skinheads in the German town where he was stationed for awhile). There should be some commonality in the papers that will help them help each other.

And what about Tom and his mirror image, Chad? They sit near the front but exhibit behavior that I usually associate with the back row—they stare off into space, occasionally put their heads on their desks, and seem to be distancing themselves as much as possible from the class. They are not disruptive, just publicly unenthused in this required course. Yet both of them write fairly well; Chad's draft is especially good. How can I get them more involved in the class? I try chatting with them in a friendly fashion before class, calling on them when they are looking out the window, standing right in front of them during discussion, and visiting briefly with their writing group (one member of which confides to me later that "all they want to do is talk about their frat parties"). Tom falls asleep one day in class. I notice, however, that Chad does contribute to class when Tom is absent. I decide to put them in separate writing groups with more enthusiastic students like Heather and An Mei; maybe their enthusiasm will be catching.

The Uses of Theory

Why do teachers of writing need to know about theories of emotion? As Tinberg and others have pointed out, some in our field see theory and teaching as separate, at odds; the two have become, in Berthoff's phrase, "killer dichotomies." As with other supposed dichotomies (affect and cognition, cognition and context), to polarize is to stigmatize, and we wind up calling each other "mere practitioners" or "ivory-tower theorists."

But theory is simply a systematic way of stating underlying principles based on available evidence. We all theorize. A class is not going well, and we ask ourselves why; we search for causes, make and test hypotheses (it must be the room, or the early hour), try new approaches. Most of the time our theories are tacit, sometimes they are incomplete and contradictory, but they are always there. A study of theory helps us address our unstated assumptions about writing and learning, helping us clarify—and modify—those assumptions; it also helps us understand our students more fully. I find it most useful to think of theory and practice not as a dichotomy but as a dialectic, interwoven and interactive: theoretical frameworks help us organize our observations in useful ways, and classroom experience pushes us to build or restructure those frameworks. Theories present us with a sense of why things happen as they do, helping us understand and sometimes predict outcomes and behaviors. For example, schema theory, described below, can help us understand one reason why a student like Alice might be so reluctant to revise her work. A writer might have a "writing the paper" schema that does not include revision as an inevitable part of the process. Once the intended action of writing the paper has—as George Mandler puts it—rushed toward completion (*Mind* 173), there is a pleasant feeling of closure; the writer reports feeling satisfied and has no urge to review what has been done, in spite of evidence that others (a peer group, the teacher) think that revision is in order. As a teacher, I find theories such as this one essential to my work, since they provide me and my students with ways of thinking about the composing process that lead to useful classroom practice (for example, discussing with Alice the fact that the "joy of completion" is a common but not entirely satisfactory response to finishing a first draft and discussing strategies to help her revise in spite of the sense of completion).

This does not mean, however, that one need subscribe only to a single theory, forsaking all others. I would not want to argue that one of the two theories under discussion in this chapter—one focusing on cognition, one on context—is "correct." They are simply the theories that have the greatest explanatory power, given the present state of theory-building in composition. They are, as the quotation from Mandler suggests in the epigraph to this chapter, simply the most convincing stories that anyone has made up so far. We need not think of them as conflicting or competing but as focusing on different phenomena. Flower has suggested that instead of striving for one "correct" view of the writing process through the lens of cognition or of context, we need a "more integrated theoretical vision which can explain how context cues cognition, which in its turn mediates and interprets the particular world that context provides" ("Cognition" 282). This chapter, then, presents two theories of emotion, one psychological, the other sociocultural, working toward a theoretical integration of cognition, context, and emotion.[1]

A Cognitive Theory of Writing

Thanks to Flower and Hayes, writing teachers are generally familiar with a cognitive approach to writing. In discussions with other teachers, however, I find that many of us are not familiar with cognitive science, especially with its research methods and the history of and assumptions behind the methods. Some information about the discipline itself is needed in order for us to understand how a cognitive theory of writing might take affect into account.

The social sciences (particularly psychology) have examined affective phenomena from varying perspectives over the last hundred years, using varied methodologies.[2] Around the turn of the century, because those who were psychologists were usually also philosophers, the method of study was introspection and self-reflection. William James is perhaps the best known of that group. During the early decades of this century, there was a reaction against such a speculative (and rather nonrigorous) model. A group of young American scientists, of whom the best known is probably B. F. Skinner, proposed instead a model for research that took into consideration only the outward manifestations of inner events—not mental processes, but the outward, measurable behaviors that were the results of those processes. Behavior provided the only valid data for scientific hypotheses; affect and cognition alike were rejected as valid concepts, since they could not be observed and measured.

But it soon became clear that the behaviorist model, while it explained some phenomena, did not explain all; humans are not merely the sum of their behaviors. With the advent of the information-processing age, scientists like Alan Newell and Herbert Simon of Carnegie-Mellon University became interested in those things the behaviorists had ignored, specifically in mental representations, in thought processes, and in problem-solving, and cognitive science was born. According to Gardner, this science has several important features, some of which are relevant to the present discussion. First, cognitive scientists based their discipline "on the assumption that, for scientific purposes, human cognitive activity must be described in terms of symbols, schemas, images, ideas, and other forms of mental representation" (39). (It may seem strange to writing teachers that one should have to justify a serious discussion of images, ideas, or symbols, but in fact it was a revolutionary idea to take mental representations as valid scientific constructs.)

At the beginning, cognitive science deemphasized such factors as context and affect. Those working to develop the discipline did not necessarily dismiss these factors, but their work was cleaner without them. It was a question of practicality. "If one were to take into account these individualizing and phenomenalistic elements, cognitive science might become impossible. In an effort to explain everything, one ends up explaining nothing" (Gardner 41). Much as the clock became a metaphor for the universe during the Enlightenment, the computer became a metaphor for human thought in cognitive science. The way that computers process, store, and retrieve information gave insight into the way the mind works; computer problem-solving (in chess games, for example) was studied for the insights it might give for human problem-solving. Comparisons of expert and novice problem-solvers pointed to successful and unsuccessful strategies. Protocol analysis (based on computer programming protocols) became a tool for research, artificial intelligence a way of looking at human intelligence, the computer program a model for human thought processes.

This computer metaphor informed the now-familiar model of the writing process first put forward by Hayes and Flower in 1980 and refined slightly in 1981 (Flower and Hayes, "Cognitive"), a model that looks rather like a flow chart for a computer program (see Figure 1).

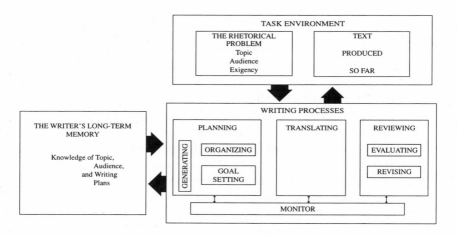

Figure 1. The structure of the writing model. From Linda Flower and John R. Hayes,"A Cognitive Process Theory of Writing," *College Composition and Communication* 32 (1981): 370. Copyright by the National Council of Teachers of English. Reprinted with permission.

The world of the writer is divided into three parts: the task environment, the writer's long-term memory (which together with the task environment constitutes the writing context), and the writing process. The latter consists of three major mental processes: planning (that is, constructing an internal representation of the knowledge needed for writing), translating (writing a draft), and reviewing (going back over what has been written). For planning, there are also the subprocesses of generating ideas, organizing those ideas, and goal setting (defining for the self both procedural and substantive goals related to the writing task); reviewing has two subprocesses, evaluating the text and revising. Controlling all these processes is a "monitor," an executive control mechanism that helps the writer determine when to move from one process to another and then back again—how long one should spend generating ideas, for example, before attempting to organize them. It is important to note two things about this model. First of all, the arrows indicate the flow of information from one process to another, not a movement of the writer from one stage to another (Flower and Hayes, "Cognitive" 386–87). The double arrows also indicate that this information flows back and forth, that the processes are recursive rather than occurring in discrete stages. Second, it should be noted that the model was developed and confirmed through observation, by analyzing think-aloud protocols from writers. In a laboratory setting, writers were asked to say out loud what they were thinking as they wrote. Their words were then transcribed and carefully analyzed, along with the resulting texts, for evidence as to their cognitive processes (see Hayes and Flower for an explanation of their procedures).

In spite of negative critiques from several quarters (Berkenkotter; Bizzell, "Cognition"; Connors, "Composition"; Cooper and Holtzman; Emig, "Inquiry Paradigms"), this theory has had an enormous impact on how the composition community views the writing process. Unlike earlier stage-process theories, it emphasizes both the recursive nature of writing and the dynamics of the process, particularly the juggling of demands and constraints (see Flower and Hayes, "Dynamics," "Cognitive"). It is also systematic, breaking down the writing process into understandable, manageable subprocesses. Comparisons between novices and experts in each of these subprocesses suggest specific strategies that novices can learn in order to improve their performance; thus the model has immediate classroom application. Flower's *Problem-Solving Strategies for Writing*, now in its fourth edition, is an elegant example of cognitive-process theory translated into practical pedagogy. Finally, the theory moves attention away from the finished product alone and focuses also on the writer's mental operations. The experimenter's relentless question "What are you thinking?" during a protocol session helps writers give glimpses of their thinking processes, somewhat like (as Hayes and Flower put it) following the tracks of a porpoise as it occasionally breaks the surface of the sea (9); the traces are incomplete, but we now have some notion about what is beneath the surface. It helps us understand the cognitive processes of a novice writer like Alice, who is unreflective about her work; she needs to develop strategic knowledge—a "monitor"—for her writing process.

Like other cognitive problem-solving models developed by researchers at Carnegie-Mellon University, this one did not address affective issues.[3] This is not to say, however, that the 1981 Flower and Hayes model is outdated and cannot still be used to explain how affect and cognition interact in the writing process. The theory of emotion formulated by George Mandler, a cognitive psychologist, can help us examine this interaction.

A Cognitive Theory of Emotion

In order to understand Mandler's theory, we need to look for a moment at how cognitive scientists discuss mental representations—how knowledge is organized and stored in the mind. The notion of the schema, first proposed by Kant in 1787 and introduced to psychology by Bartlett in 1932, was developed by cognitive scientists into a theory of how knowledge is represented and used; schemas are units of thought, the building blocks of cognition.[4] They are the mental elements that interpret sensory data, retrieve information from memory, organize actions, determine goals, and generally guide the flow of mental processing (Rumelhart 33–34).[5] Theorists use the analogy of a play to describe the characteristics of schemas. Just as a play has roles that can be filled with various actors in different performances, so a schema has variables that are defined by particular instances, or "instantiations," of that schema (see Rumelhart and Ortony 101). The schema for "write," for example, usually involves the variables of writer, the act of writing, the written product, and a reader. There are different kinds of schemas; of most interest for this discussion are the event schemas, those representations that organize common sequences of events temporally. They may be thought of as a set of expectations about what will occur in a given situation (see J. Mandler, "Categorical" 11). The organization of these event schemas drives us to complete them in sequence. So powerful is this drive toward completion that we will try to complete our plans or planned behavior even when we cannot (like Ed trying to log on to the computer network using the same failed strategy, over and over), or we will complete plans in what turns out to be an unsatisfactory way just to come to closure and then resist going back to change anything (like Alice, who resisted revising).

The interruption of plans or planned behavior is central to Mandler's theory (outlined in *Mind and Body*) of how emotions occur. Like several other cognitive theorists (Schachter and Singer; Lazarus, Kanner, and Folkman; Averill, "Constructivist"), Mandler holds that an emotional experience involves both mind and body. It is constructed out of two elements: arousal of the autonomic nervous system (the visceral reaction—a quickened heartbeat, a tensing of muscles) and a cognitive—but not necessarily conscious— evaluation of that arousal (a negative or positive interpretation of the physical reaction, labeling it as "fear," "joy," "frustration," and the like). The cognitive evaluation is crucial to the experience of the emotion. Bertrand Russell, reflecting about his experience with being injected with epinephrine (adrenaline), wrote that he felt the bodily reactions of an emotion but did not really experience an emotion: he felt *as if* he were fearful but knew there was no reason for such an emotion. Russell concluded that without a cognitive element, there is no emotion (218–19). We experience emotions physically; we construct them mentally.

What accounts for the visceral arousal that needs interpretation? According to Mandler, we experience the feelings of emotion when the expectations of some schema are violated—when there is a discrepancy in what we think will happen and what actually happens, when some action is interrupted, when ongoing plans are blocked. (Note that Mandler does not say that emotions *are* interruptions but that interruptions, blocks, or novel situations—such as the situation Ed found himself in while trying to log on to the computer network—are the *occasions* for arousal of the autonomic nervous system.) This theory, based on the interruption of schemas, fits the cognitive model of the writing process. In "Plans That Guide the Composing Process," Flower and Hayes describe the range of mental operations that comprise the writing process: forming an internal representation of your writing task, defining goals and strategies, and then during the writing itself assessing your progress and "with disturbing frequency" (40) redefining your goals to fit the multiple constraints of audience, rhetorical situation, topic knowledge, and the discourse conventions of written prose (see "Dynamics" 34–40; Cleary has shown how often various student writers experience such interruptions and how they react to them). In other words, interruption of plans—a major reason for emotions to occur, according to Mandler—is an integral part of the writing process Flower and Hayes have described. Affect and cognition are inseparable as we write.[6]

What seems crucial for teachers to understand, as I have discussed elsewhere ("Some Thoughts"), is the cognitive interpretation of the sensory data generated by the interruption of plans. When I am working on a project like this book,

I find the flow of thoughts continually interrupted by the constraints of audience and topic knowledge (Will teachers get something out of the information on psychological theories? Have I represented the various psychological theories adequately and fairly?). Observers would note evidence of a certain amount of visceral tension as I write—I type for awhile, get up and pace, then sit back down at the computer. But because I am intrigued by and engaged in my subject, I evaluate the tension as interest, even excitement. Likewise, when I experience a feeling of relaxation and satisfaction following a particularly intense writing session, I do not interpret those feelings to mean that I am finished with the written product, since I know about the cycles of tension and relaxation (described by Bloom and Broder) involved in problem-solving. I am conscious of my emotional states, and they aid my writing and revision processes.

Watch student writers at work and you will also see signs of autonomic arousal—they wad paper, sigh, run their hands through their hair, chew on pencils. How do they interpret their tension? Larson investigated a number of high school students engaged in a long writing project, finding that the students could be sorted into two groups. The first group found their emotional states disruptive. Some in this group (like Leontina trying to write about the racial incident in her high school) were overaroused and overanxious; even though they were interested in their topics, they found it hard to focus, sometimes working themselves into a frenzy. Others in this group (like Alice) were underaroused, bored, disinterested; they were not engaged at all in their task. The papers of both the overaroused and the underaroused students were judged by independent raters to be fragmented, disjointed, mechanical. These findings conform to the Yerkes-Dodson Law, which suggests an inverted U-shaped relationship between arousal and performance on laboratory tasks—that is, both high and low arousal interferes with the subjects' ability to cope with task requirements; those in the middle, like the students described below, were best able to cope with the task. (See Yerkes and Dodson; G. Mandler, *Mind* 226). This might be thought of as the "Goldilocks Law": in order to perform well on a task, one should be in an emotional state that is not too hot, not too cold, but just right.[7]

The second group of students in Larson's study were in that "just right" condition where their emotions were enabling. They were interested in their projects, sometimes becoming so absorbed as they wrote that they lost track of time. In describing their emotional state, some students used the word "flow," a state studied by Csikszentmihalyi where there appears to be a balance between the perceived challenge of the task and the person's skills (*Beyond, Flow*). Although the students in the second group were no different from those in the first in terms of their scores on achievement tests and their experience with writing long assignments, their resulting papers were judged by raters to be appreciably better than those of the other group. What is interesting about this group of students, as Larson notes, is that they appeared to be using deliberate strategies to engage and then control their emotions (34-36): they worked at making the task enjoyable, monitored their internal states and their energy levels, stopped themselves when they got overexcited, and generally tried to adjust the balance between the challenge and their skills. In other words, they used metaaffective as well as metacognitive strategies for writing, controlling their affective state so that it was "just right" for writing.

Larson's research suggests some classroom applications of Mandler's theory. There has been much attention given recently to improving learning skills through encouraging metacognition—helping students know *how* to know. The research conducted by Faigley and his colleagues implies that one way we can help students with their writing is to increase their awareness of their own composing processes. Experienced writers, according to this research, have a well-developed executive mental mechanism (the "monitor" of the Flower and Hayes model) that helps them track their progress, allowing them to step back from their work to assess it.

If we can use these expert strategies as models for students, it follows that we can also use the experts' meta-affective monitoring strategies as models for novices. We can tell students like Leontina, for example, of the strategies used by the students in Larson's study. We can tell them that all writers experience feelings of tension and that they can learn to interpret tension (and the ensuing relaxation once the paper is finished) in an enabling rather than in a debilitating way. Teaching people to change their cognitive interpretation of sensory data is not a novel idea; the medical profession has been using the technique for some time—dentists now routinely tell their patients not to mistake pressure for pain. The technique works. A study of a particularly uncomfortable medical test found that patients who were told what bodily sensations to expect during the test and how to interpret what was happening were able to process those sensations as "normal" rather than threatening (Johnson and Leventhal). It follows that we could ask students like Alice and Leontina not only what they are thinking but also how they are feeling as they write: do they need to calm down or pump up? We can then help them work out specific monitoring and coping strategies for those internal states—affective as well as cognitive—working toward strategic self-management in both domains.

An excellent model for helping students become aware of and manage their affective states may be found in Vivian Rosenberg's composition textbook, *Reading, Writing, and Thinking: Critical Connections*. In chapter 2 of this book, "Thinking about Feelings," Rosenberg first explains to students how their thoughts and feelings are intertwined and how they need to be aware of their own and others' feelings if they are to be good critical thinkers and writers (in order to think about audience one has to be able to understand the feelings of that audience). She then discusses how to recognize and describe emotion—how to interpret the visceral feel-

ings—supplying lists students can use for such interpretation and exercises to help them use the lists. In the summary
at the end of the chapter, she tells students how understanding the emotional dimension of their experience will help
them, advising them to learn to recognize and accept how
they feel as they approach an assignment, to give themselves
permission to experience confusion, to use the problem-solving strategies in other chapters to get over the confusion or
to get them engaged if they are bored, and to use their empathic capacity as they develop audience awareness (45).
These nuggets of advice are then expanded upon with examples in the chapters on writing and on reading strategies,
combining instruction on cognitive and affective processes.

Social Construction Theories of Writing

Let us now examine composition and the emotions
through the lens of social constructionist theory. The cognitive theory of writing examines how the mind represents
knowledge to itself; social construction theory examines how
those representations are shaped by context, by the conventions and expectations of particular social and cultural
groups.[8] Vygotsky suggested that individual consciousness
is built not from within but from without, through social relationships; communication with others is internalized, becoming the "inner speech" that is vital to thought. Social
constructionists build on Vygotsky's idea of construction,
holding that knowledge itself, as well as the individual consciousness, is constructed.

Thomas Kuhn's *Structure of Scientific Revolutions*, a book
that challenged conventional assumptions about the nature
of scientific knowledge, is singled out by Kenneth Bruffee
("Collaborative," "Social") as the work that heralded social
construction theory. Scientific knowledge, Kuhn held, is not
discovered so much as built collectively by the scientific community; changes in how this community views phenomena

occur not because of a further accumulation of data but because of the way scientists agree collectively to interpret the data. According to Bruffee, Kuhn's ideas were generalized by philosopher Richard Rorty in his *Philosophy and the Mirror of Nature;*[9] Rorty discussed knowledge in all fields as a social artifact, as socially justified belief. We arrive at a consensus about this belief—about what constitutes knowledge in our fields—through disciplinary "conversations," both written and oral. These rather specialized conversations about knowledge in a particular field help to constitute a "discourse community," a group that has particular rules for the conversation: a specialized vocabulary, certain rhetorical conventions that are valued (such as conciseness in the sciences), certain ways of talking about knowledge that seem so natural to those in the community that they often forget how strange they may be to those outside the community. For example, the graduate students in the American studies program at my institution often have difficulty shifting discourse when they move from literature to history seminars. One of these students helped me understand one of the reasons for the difficulty—the verb tenses.[10] In literature, the discourse accepts the use of present tense when one is quoting the words of long-dead authors; since Shakespeare is not of an age but for all time, we can write "Shakespeare says." In history, however, one could never write "Gibbon says"; when quoting from past sources in that field, one must put them in their historical context. To use the present tense is to imply not that your source is timeless but that he or she is still alive.

If knowledge is socially constructed in the conversations of discourse communities, it follows that one of the things teachers need to do is recognize the difficulty of learning all these specialized forms of discourse and demystify them for students. We can help students succeed by introducing them first to generalized academic discourse (see Bizzell, "College"; Bartholomae) and then as they move into their chosen disciplines, the more specialized discourse of those fields.

Using the tools of discourse analysis they learn in our classes, students should not only be able to understand the varied conversations in academe but also be equipped to deal with other specialized discourses they may encounter after they leave our halls. We can also introduce them to the collaborative processes at work in the construction of knowledge through collaborative learning and writing tasks in the classroom. The use of writing groups in various configurations and permutations (pairs of students involved in collaborative planning, several students working together on a single text, a peer tutor in a writing lab working with several students) is the most visible classroom manifestation of this theory.

Those who write about social construction and the teaching of writing usually discuss just the aspects of social constructive process mentioned above: writing as creating a discourse community and as a form of social behavior within that community or discipline. But there is another process at work as well: writers construct mental representations of the social contexts for their writing, for example, when they consider audience and purpose (see Rubin 2). Students must learn not only to analyze discourse but also to mentally represent ways of situating themselves in that discourse. If we consider a constructivist theory of writing to include mental representations of social context, that theory complements rather than contradicts cognitive-process writing theory.

A Sociocultural Theory of the Emotions

We may also think of a social constructionist theory of emotion as complementary to cognitive process theories of emotion.[11] We have already seen that cognitive theories such as George Mandler's take as a given the individual construction of affective states. But we can also think of emotional states as socially determined constructions, shaped by particular contexts and cultures (like a university or a particular classroom).

Those who write about the social construction of the emotions are opposed to the traditional view, traceable to Darwin, that emotional responses are essentially biological in origin, hardwired into the organism in the course of evolution (for an explanation of this view see Izard; Tomkins). Social construction theorists do not deny that some emotions, like fear, seem innate. However, they see most emotional response as shaped by the environment rather than biologically determined; the instinctive responses of infants (smiling or crying) *become* expressions of emotion in a societal context (De Sousa 285). Our capacity to experience emotions such as shame, guilt, or love is contingent upon our internalization of cultural norms and principles (Armon-Jones). The cognitive appraisal of physiological data, which figures so importantly in cognitive-process models of emotion, also looms large here. Sociocultural theories of emotion conclude that such appraisal is shaped socially as well as individually, conditioned by the norms and standards of our culture.

These theorists point to the cultural variations among emotional constructs as proof of their notion that affective response is culturally shaped rather than biologically determined. In Japan, for example, there is an emotion for which Western society has no specific equivalent—*amae*, variously translated as "to play baby" or "to depend or presume upon another's love," carrying connotations of sweetness and permissiveness as well as closeness to a loved one (Morsbach and Tyler). Western notions of "regression" or "infantilism" suggest the reason why we have no exact synonym; it is connected to behavior our society does not sanction. In Castillian Spanish, *coraje* connotes aggressiveness, while in English, "courage" need not include that trait (Crespo). As further proof of their theory, social constructionists also point to changes in emotional constructs over time. Guilt to the ancient Greek, for example, had little to do with willful action or sin; it was contamination, often as the result of acts against the gods committed unknowingly, as in the case of Oedipus

(Heelas). The emotion "accidie," common in medieval times, occurred when one did not do one's duty to God with joy and delight; those who most experienced the state were hermits who became bored with their ascetic life (Harré and Finlay-Jones). Along with hermits, the emotion is now rare.

One issue of interest in the sociocultural theory of emotion is that it allows us to think of emotions in dramatistic terms, as transitory social roles in the plot structures of culture (see Sarbin; Averill, "Constructivist"). For example, the role that the angry person is allowed or expected to play can vary greatly from culture to culture; extreme examples are the "wild man" behavior of some New Guinea Highlanders and the phenomenon of "amok" (aggressive frenzy, as in "running amok") in several Southeast Asian societies (Averill, *Anger* 55–63. (One thinks about the well-documented phenomenon of binge drinking among college students and the "boys will be boys" role that intoxicated students have been allowed to play in American culture.) The repertoire of dramatistic emotional roles one can play is learned from what one theorist calls "paradigm scenarios" (De Sousa 285). These scenarios are prototypes of the social drama and are learned early in life—children play at being angry or fearful, just as they play at being parents or doctors, as they work to understand the meaning of the emotional roles they observe (Averill, "Constructivist" 321). Various cultural myths, beliefs, and values give shape to the roles. Anger, for example, is shaped by "courtroom or Olympian mythology; oneself as legislator or judge; the other as defendant. Oneself as the defender of values, the other as offender" (Solomon 289). In writing groups we ask students to play the role of coach, one that has important emotional components; we can teach them how to play this role effectively through observation and modeling—for example, by using a "fishbowl" of volunteers or a videotape of an exemplary writing group (like the award-winning *Student Writing Groups: Demonstrating the Process*).

The immediate social context for the cognitive appraisal of the emotional experience also has an effect on that appraisal. Laughter is heartier in the presence of other happy persons, for example; fear is "contagious," as is the calming influence of companions who are not afraid. The classic experiments by Schachter and Singer, which suggested the importance of cognitive appraisal, also suggested the contextual aspects of emotional reactions. The experimenters injected epinephrine (adrenaline) into their subjects; some were told that this injection would produce increased heartbeat and physical tension, and some were not. Each subject was then placed in a room with another person who had also supposedly received an injection. Actually, the second person in the room was a shill, employed by the experimenters. In one condition of the experiment, the shill feigned euphoria, floating paper airplanes, playing with a hula hoop, and shooting wads of paper. In the other, the actor feigned anger while filling out a questionnaire, finally tearing it up and stalking from the room. Those subjects who had been informed of the physiological reaction from the injection had no emotional reaction to their companions' behavior. Those who had not been informed, however, took on the emotion of the actor in the room with them—they became either angry or euphoric. In other words, since they did not know the reason for their visceral arousal, they interpreted it in light of the available social data. Averill points out that physical surroundings (what he terms the "environmental psychology of the emotions") can have an effect on cognitive interpretation as well; it is easier to become angry in a bar than in a church, to be frightened at night than during the day, to become jovial at a party than in the classroom ("Constructivist" 323). Thus the emotions involve not only a cognitive evaluation of physiological arousal (an evaluation shaped by cultural and social norms and expectations) but also of the particular social setting in which one experiences that visceral arousal.

How can an understanding of the social construction of the emotions help us in the composition classroom? First of all, such an understanding will show us how important the environmental psychology of the classroom can be in determining students' affective responses to writing. (Such a concern may seem trivial, but those who arrange professional conferences know how important it is to the success of their gatherings to have pleasant hotel accommodations and meeting rooms.) We can't always change from one room to another, as I did, but we can do other small things—put the chairs in a circle, erase a blackboard full of mathematical symbols from a previous class, bring coffee, turn on all the lights—that can have a noticeable impact on the classroom atmosphere. It is also important that the teacher establish a particular persona at the beginning of the semester; the effect of teacher affect will be discussed in a later chapter, but for now it should be noted that whatever their methods, successful teachers appear confident and competent, make their concern for students apparent, and express their confidence that students can perform at the level expected (Spear). Teachers can do much at the beginning of the semester to establish a classroom atmosphere that fosters facilitative emotional reactions to writing.

Group work, as Gere has pointed out, can do much to encourage a positive attitude toward writing. Students can share their emotional as well as their cognitive writing experiences and strategies with one another, coming to understand that their reactions are not unique. The decision to put Leontina in a group with others who had written about racial incidents they had found disturbing and personally threatening was guided by the notion that they could help one another if they shared their emotional reactions as well as their papers. Their first session turned out to be so successful from their point of view that they asked to stay together for the next paper; while Leontina's paper was not the best of the group, she was able to improve upon her first draft after seeing how Ed's and Alberto's papers dealt with similar issues. Putting Tom and Chad in separate groups also had a salutary effect. They no longer had another person next to them to validate and mirror their behavior, and while Tom continued to be detached, Chad became much more engaged—even helpful—when in his writing group. He seemed to be pulled into the higher level of enthusiasm exhibited by the other students in the group.

There are other ways in which an understanding of the social construction of emotions can help us as teachers. If it is true that our emotions are shaped in part by "paradigm scenarios," then we can try to learn more about those scenarios. We can, for instance, have our students write in their journals or in inksheddings about the emotions they experienced in certain paradigmatic writing situations (writing a piece and then getting the paper back from the teacher, for example) and discuss what influence they think those emotions might continue to have on their writing.[12] If we agree that our emotions are shaped by our culture, we also need to examine how that culture views writing and what cultural myths or beliefs might help shape the emotional roles we play when we write (see Gere and Smith). Beliefs and attitudes are the subject of another chapter, but two examples here will serve to make the point. The first is belief in the romantic myth that writing results only from bursts of creative inspiration. The muse visits, you write, and the result of your first draft is "Kubla Khan." Preparation and revision are obviously unnecessary. With this kind of myth helping to shape our emotional reactions to writing, it is no wonder that many of us (not just students) get discouraged waiting for inspiration to strike, or that we resent having to revise our work if we feel inspiration has produced it. We must make explicit to students that the myth of inspiration is just that; few writers, including Coleridge, ever wrote polished and complete first drafts. Students can learn (as discussed in chapter 5) to make an appointment with the muse, to establish writing habits that give them time to draft and revise and thus not be distressed when a piece doesn't turn out well the first time.

The second cultural belief that we need to deal with is that for those not blessed with creativity, learning to write is a technical rather than an intellectual process, that the job of the writing teacher is to hunt down error, that revision is simply clearing a paper of such error, that teaching grammar is equivalent to teaching writing. (This belief is closely connected to the value our culture places on correctness and appearance.) Our professional journals testify to the fact that we have exploded this myth, but it persists—as myths do—in the culture, sometimes as close as the next classroom. This myth helps explain some students' frustration over that fact that we *don't* cover their papers with red ink, since that is what they expect as a result of their past experience. It also helps us understand their negative attitude when we ask them to rethink the whole paper rather than just tinkering with surface features in their revisions. To counteract such an attitude, we can show students examples of professional writers revising and share with them our struggles with our own writing, helping them understand what is involved in reseeing a paper rather than simply editing it.

Finally, to return to the uses of theory, we can as teachers do what we ask our students to do about the writing process: observe (and ask others to observe) our own teaching and our students' learning processes; reflect systematically and regularly in a teaching journal about classroom events and interactions with students; and try—as Mandler suggests in the epigraph to this chapter—to make up stories about teaching and learning that make comprehensible the evidence at hand. Those stories will be most convincing if they are grounded in theory.

❦ 3 ❦

Motivation and Writing

The chief impediments to learning are not cognitive.
It is not that students cannot learn; it is that they do
not wish to. If educators invested a fraction of the
energy they now spend trying to transmit information
in trying to stimulate the students' enjoyment of
learning, we could achieve much better results.
          —Mihaly Csikszentmihalyi,
          "Literacy and Intrinsic Motivation"

We are getting close to the midterm "dry-run" portfolio readings for the class. My students will have their papers read by one of my colleagues and rated either as
"passing" or "needs improvement." No grades will be attached to these portfolio readings, but it is still a high-stakes
situation; students who do not receive a rating of "passing"
on their portfolios at the end of the semester will not pass
the class. This situation—having my students' ultimate fate
in this class being in the hands of someone else—has the
advantage of making me more of a coach than a judge of
their work, but it does create some anxiety. To further com-
plicate the grading situation, while I do grade each student's
collective work at midterm and at the end of the course, I do
not grade individual student papers, trying to provide what
Elbow calls an "evaluation-free zone" ("Ranking"). I want
students to focus for now on how to make their writing better, not on what grade they got or want to get. For the most

part they accept my explanations of my grading and of the portfolio system, and in spite of the fact that such activity does not promise a higher grade, they are busily revising their papers for the midterm "practice" portfolio reading.

At least, most of them are. Four provide some interesting contrasts in terms of their motivation, however. Alice and An Mei are at about the same level in terms of their writing skills (and are in the same tutorial group outside class). Alice, who has continued to have trouble revising to make her paper more analytical, is nervous about the lack of grades—she tells me she is used to knowing "where she stands" and is worried about failing. I tell her she can come in to talk to me at any time and I will try to let her know how she is doing, so she comes, often. I find out during these conferences that she can't see the point of the reading journal I have asked students to keep, since it doesn't receive a letter grade. The portfolio, with its possibility of failure, frightens her, and she feels "stressed" about getting her papers ready for a reader she doesn't know. When the midterm reading for her portfolio comes back positive, however, she is relieved, and her visits to my office stop. Even though there are suggestions from the reader for strengthening the paper, she decides not to change anything. Why revise when the paper passed?

An Mei, another frequent visitor to my office, views the midterm portfolio quite differently. She tells me that it provides her with a good chance to revise her papers "precisely"; she comes for several consultations and works diligently with her tutorial group, revising many times. She says that she feels proud of the result when she turns it in. Her portfolio passes but receives some fairly negative comments on her cultural encounter paper, which describes how she improved her English when she first came to this country by watching TV commercials. The reader urged her to be more critical of American culture, particularly of its consumerism. This reaction mystifies and upsets her, but she seems spurred on by the comments. How can she revise to make a reader other than me understand that she needed work on idiomatic English and that TV commercials helped her more than textbooks with the spoken idiom? Unlike Alice, she is eager to rework her passing paper, wanting very much to improve her skills.

Then there is baby-faced Ira. His matter-of-factness about not being good in English has given way to a hangdog expression and a complete lack of effort. His first freewrite consisted of two sentences: "I can't do this. I don't know what you mean by freewrite." His first draft consists of a rumpled page of notes, without a coherent sentence in sight. He tells me that the readings are "too hard"; that's why he has nothing to say in class. I wonder if he might have a learning disability, but he tells me he has been tested and does not; he doesn't have a problem—my class is the problem. With the help of his writing group, he does finally struggle and produce a draft of a paper on his encounter with the strange culture of college. It has some promising ideas, and I make a point of praising it to him—even reading bits of it aloud to the class. But he puts off revising it and has to turn it in unrevised for the midterm portfolio reading. He also does not write a cover letter for the portfolio and does not include the in-class essay, as required, since he "lost" it. His portfolio fails, primarily because he has not put forth any effort. His reaction—"I knew it would fail. Like I said, I've never been good at English."

Will is also struggling. His first effort at a freewrite was, like Ira's, short and labored. But he is a reader who wants to write—Updike, Steinbeck, and Hemingway are his favorite authors, he tells me, and he would like to model his writing after theirs. He has high aspirations. I ask him if he has heard of writer's block (he has not, but he nods in assent when I describe the phenomenon), and we discuss how others, including his favorite authors, have dealt with it. I notice that he mumbles to himself as he writes; he says he "talks himself through" ideas in order to keep writing. I ask him to share some of his subvocalizations with me as he works on a piece, and I discover that besides mulling over ideas he is using a sort of pep-talk strategy to keep himself on task ("I'm sick of this paper but I need to go on—if I stop now I'll never get back into it—OK, where was I?"). We discuss a few other strategies he can use and other techniques besides self-coaching for what he terms "fighting a paper," like setting aside a particular time to write. I agree to extend deadlines for him if need be. He finally produces a paper describing and analyzing his encounters with Native American culture while growing up in a small Montana town. It's the most sophisticated piece of analysis I've seen from a freshman; his portfolio receives high praise from the anonymous reader, who suggests that he submit it to the campus literary magazine. Still, Will is not satisfied with the paper and wants to continue to work on it. Writing does not come easily for him, but he seems to be such a high achiever that he is willing to take on the struggle.

Four students, four widely different pictures of motivation. No wonder motivation is something of a mystery to teachers. Why is it that some of our students (like Alice) seem so apathetic about improving their writing, while others who are no better in terms of ability are (like An Mei) eager to learn and work hard on improving their skills? Why do some students (like Ira) give up when a task becomes challenging while others (like Will) persist at the same task, struggling in spite of difficulty and meeting the challenge? What should we as teachers do to keep eager students motivated and to energize those who need to be more motivated? This chapter aims at making motivation a little less mysterious, something that teachers can understand and take into account as they work with student writers.

"Motivation" comes from the Latin *movere*, to move; the concept embraces all the factors that move us to engage in and direct our behavior in purposeful ways, to set goals and then strive to reach those goals. Exactly how we are motivated and can work to motivate others is not always well understood, however. As Dweck points out, recent research has called into question several commonsense notions about motivation and learning: that children's natural urge to learn would continue unabated if not sabotaged by the evaluative practices of formal schooling; that large amounts of praise and success will help motivate students; that brighter students are more likely to choose challenging tasks or to persist when a task becomes difficult. In fact, Dweck asserts, schools may not squelch students' natural enthusiasm for learning so much as fail to teach new sets of skills and foster new motivational frameworks for working on intellectual tasks; the lavishing of praise as a reinforcement tactic (as I tried with Ira) may not increase the probability that students will seek out learning tasks with confidence or persist when the tasks become difficult; and brighter students, especially females, are not necessarily more motivated to seek challenges or to persist in the face of difficulties ("Motivation" 88, 97). The situation is rather more complex than Csikszentmihalyi's statement, the epigraph to this chapter, suggests.

What Motivates Our Students? Some Perspectives

Motivation, like emotion, has been studied from a number of different perspectives. Before the beginnings of modern psychology, motivation was referred to as "will"; as the term implies, a certain freedom informed the construct—individuals had some control over their goals and could direct their behavior willfully. One could choose to write sonnets, lead a religious reform movement, or study the stars and planets. Freud's instinct theory and Hull's later (1941) behaviorist drive theory changed that view, however; people were thought to do things not because they wanted to but because they had to—they were not moved so much as driven to action. Individuals, both these theories contended, strive to reduce internal tension and reach equilibrium, or homeostasis. The fundamental motivational principle was that any

deviation from equilibrium provides a force to satisfy biological needs and return to internal balance (Weiner, *Theories*)—hunger drives us to eat, aggression to fight, sexual
energy to mate.[1] Along with the principle of homeostasis, a
fundamental axiom of these theories was hedonism—organ-
isms strive to avoid pain and increase pleasure. Reward and
punishment were the only external motivating factors.

Ironically enough, it was behaviorist research that began to change this notion of motivation. Researchers found
that laboratory rats and monkeys behaved in certain ways
not just to return to equilibrium but to seek challenging tasks,
to explore new territory, to see new sights (Harlow;
Csikszentmihalyi and Nakamura 46). Psychologists had to
add competency, curiosity, and novelty to the list of drives
that motivated behavior (White; Butler). Motivational theory
made room for the "optimal arousal" hypothesis: that or-
ganisms had a need not only for homeostasis but also for
additional stimulation when understimulated (Hebb;
Berlyne; Day, Berlyne, and Hunt). The rigid link between
what happened biologically and what the organism did began to weaken; as theories became less mechanistic, a certain amount of freedom and ability to control crept back into
the concept of motivation (Csikszentmihalyi and Nakamura
46). Psychologists began to speak of extrinsic motivation
(related to stimulus-response learning from reward or punishment—Alice's need for grades, for example) and intrinsic
motivation (related to some goal-related decision of the individual rather than external reward or punishment, such
as Will's desire to be a writer).

Intrinsic and Extrinsic Motivation

With the concepts of intrinsic and extrinsic motivation,
we move to a more social view of the phenomenon. What
moved people to action was the desire to be effective in
changing their environment in some way, to be masters of

their fates, captains of their souls. Some of the earliest work in this area was done by deCharms, who discussed motivation in terms of what he called "origin" and "pawn" behavior: origins are those persons who see their behavior as determined by their own choosing, while pawns see their behavior as determined by external forces beyond their control (*Personal Causation* 273–74). If people see their behavior resulting from their own choice, they value the results of that behavior, but if they see the same behavior resulting from the dictates of an outside force, they devalue the same behavior and its results. (This explains why student evaluations of required classes are invariably lower than of electives, even though students might do well in both classes.) Play, as deCharms points out, becomes work if forced; if one can choose one's work without regard to outside forces, it becomes play, rewarding in and of itself (273). The theory was put to the test during the mid-1960s, when deCharms worked with inner-city schoolchildren and their teachers on a program designed to enhance the motivation of both groups. After this experience, the theory was refined; the difference between origins and pawns came to be seen not as a difference between freedom and constraint but as a difference in outlook. The origin (like An Mei or Will) is able to determine personally meaningful goals within constraints, while the pawn (like Alice or Ira) sees only the constraints. Origins take personal responsibility for their actions, for their learning; pawns do not (*Enhancing Motivation* 205–09).

What is interesting about deCharms's work is that he found that students could be taught to distinguish between controllable and uncontrollable outcomes and to set realistic goals based on their own probability of success. They learned to see goals as challenges rather than threats, to take responsibility for their own learning. As the students trained in the program increased their motivation, their academic achievement also rose (141–60). Pawns, in other words, can learn to be origins. This transformation seems to be best accomplished in a warmly supportive classroom atmosphere where the teacher respects the students and treats them as capable of guiding their own behavior—treats everyone, in effect, like an origin (66). This research suggests that the student-centered, collaborative classroom that most composition pedagogy values is the right atmosphere for increasing student motivation. It also suggests that we would do well to make motivational concepts explicit to students and to help those who seem to have pawn-like tendencies to set and accomplish realistic goals for themselves.

The concept of intrinsic motivation took a new turn when several researchers began to examine how extrinsic reinforcers (those staples of behaviorist theory) actually undermined intrinsically motivated behavior. Again, this new turn began in the behaviorist's lab. Harlow noticed that monkeys manipulated puzzles without being rewarded for the activity, but once the puzzles were baited with a reward (a raisin), the monkeys lost interest in unbaited puzzles. It seemed that an extrinsic reward, when added to an ongoing intrinsically motivated activity, reduced the subject's interest in the activity for its own sake (deCharms, *Personal Causation*). Extrinsic rewards did not enhance but actually replaced intrinsic motivation. This might explain the behavior of students like Alice—grades and the approval of a known authority figure (a teacher, a tutor, a portfolio reader) become more important than the learning that the grades are supposed to measure. Extrinsic rewards had become the major motivating force in her academic life.

Further experiments documented some of the conditions under which rewards decreased individuals' interest in certain activities. One experiment found that if people received money for engaging in activities they enjoyed, they lost interest in those activities faster than when they were not rewarded (Deci, "Effects"). In a study involving college students, researchers found that subjects chose challenging puzzles until money was introduced as a reward; then the subjects chose the easiest puzzles to ensure receiving the reward (Shapira). If the reward was introduced in one period, the subjects chose easier puzzles in a subsequent period when rewards were no longer offered (Pittman, Emery, and Boggiano). Researchers suggested that situations enhancing intrinsic motivation include self-determined behavior or choice, positive feedback, and optimally challenging activities; those that decrease intrinsic motivation include external rewards or pressures to act in particular ways, feedback that implies external rather than internal reasons for success, and ego-involving task conditions that might challenge self-esteem (Ryan, Connell, and Deci). More recently researchers have revised this situational model, saying that it is not just the situation itself but also the individual's perception of the situation that enhances or decreases intrinsic motivation. Individuals can react very differently to the same situational cues (see Dweck, "Intrinsic Motivation" 296). Much of the research on the effects of reward systems on intrinsic motivation has been summarized in a volume with the rather ominous title *The Hidden Costs of Reward* (Lepper and Greene).[2]

What does this line of research imply for that mother of all academic reward systems, grades? First of all, it does not imply that we should entirely do away with grades as a motivating factor—extrinsic rewards can still be useful methods of motivating behavior, especially with those students like Alice for whom intrinsic motivation is not great or who do not have strong feelings of competence and self-determination (Lepper and Greene 142). It seemed very necessary for her to come to my office periodically and be reassured about where she stood. And as Lepper and Hodell point out, it may not be possible to experience the intrinsic satisfaction of some academic tasks until one has acquired a certain level of proficiency, and extrinsic rewards can be useful to get students to that level (88). But the research on intrinsic motivation suggests that we do need to think carefully about how grades might be used and exactly what they might motivate students to do. For example, Lepper and Greene state that the explicit use of extrinsic rewards (like grades) to modify behavior brings up the issues of control and volition. These issues can influence an individual's perception of an activity's intrinsic value, resulting in that person not wanting to engage in the activity in the absence of the rewards (xi). Too much emphasis on grades in a writing class could cause students to devalue the activity of writing when it is not being graded (as in writing-to-learn activities) or to lose interest in self-sponsored writing.

Lepper and Greene also state that the promise of an extrinsic reward tends to focus an individual's attention only on the aspects of performance that are directly related to the attainment of that reward (xi). Many teachers who want to motivate students to revise their work promise higher grades for revision, only to find that students will do a minimal revision and then expect an "A" for their effort; the teacher's bid to engage the student in revision has actually focused that student's attention on revising for the grade rather than on rethinking the ideas in the paper. Separating revision from grading (for example, by grading only when the student and teacher agree that a paper is ready and then moving on to revising the next draft, or by grading the body of a student's work in a portfolio) would focus the student's motivation more on overall improvement than on a reward for a specific revision task.

Achievement Motivation

Achievement motivation presents us with a slightly different perspective on students' engagement with their writing.[3] The research on intrinsic motivation highlights how perceived control can determine task persistence; achievement motivation theories examine perceived ability or competence in achievement situations. There are three achievement theories that are of interest here: need achievement, test anxiety, and attribution theory, a subset of which involves a phenomenon known as "learned helplessness."

The first theory to conceptualize achievement motivation was put forward by McClelland and his associates in the early 1950s and was built around the notion of the need to achieve and display competence. These researchers postulated two acquired drives they called "motives": one to achieve success, the other to avoid failure. These motives were thought to be acquired through conditioning in achievement situations where children learned to feel pride in accomplishment and shame at failure, emotions that fostered approach or avoidance behavior toward later tasks. Thus affect played a large role in this early theory even though it was developed within a behaviorist framework—one's affective state as one anticipated achievement goals was seen as the energizing force behind approach or avoidance in achievement situations. The motive to achieve success involved positive anticipation about goals, an expressed desire to do a good job, an emphasis on tasks as a means to success, and positive emotions associated with striving to achieve goals. The motive to avoid failure was seen not as driving people toward success but as inhibiting their achievement activities; this motive involved anxiety about doing a poor job, expressions of inadequacy ("I've never been good at English"), an emphasis on the difficulty of tasks ("The readings are too hard"), and negative emotions associated with evaluative situations. People like Will who have a strong need to achieve will take on challenging tasks, while people like Alice who have a strong need to avoid failure avoid challenge unless there are strong extrinsic rewards.

Test anxiety theory, like need achievement theory, assumes that acquired drives can energize or inhibit performance; the theory was also developed in the 1950s by, among others, George Mandler. Test anxiety is defined as a drive acquired in achievement situations that facilitates or inhibits performance on evaluative tasks (Mandler and Sarason). This theory is the foundation for the studies of writing anxiety (or writing apprehension), begun as a part of Daly and Miller's research on communication apprehension.

Both need achievement and test anxiety theory have come under fire recently (see Dweck and Elliott 648–50). George Mandler, speaking with special privilege by virtue of his role as one of the theory's founders, opines that research on test anxiety has been noncumulative, contributing to a kind of "dustbowl empiricism" in which the production of data becomes more important than the development of a determinate theory ("Helplessness" 361–64). Others have criticized the theories for emphasizing only the negative, debilitating effects of affect, when it seems that affect can also be enabling; as Bannister has shown, some level of apprehension actually aids writing in the planning stages. The theories also ignore the possibility that cognition as well as affect might influence the formation of achievement expectancies (Weiner, *Theories*). Nevertheless, both theories are important in that they have established various constructs for discussion and research. The differentiation between state anxiety and trait anxiety in determining test anxiety, for example, is a useful one. State anxiety is situation-specific, occurring only in achievement or testing situations; trait anxiety describes an individual's reaction to all the stresses of everyday life (see Spielberger). Our interventions as teachers are much more likely to be successful with the student (like Will) who is anxious only in achievement situations than with the student who is anxious about everything (the latter might need to talk to a counselor rather than to a composition teacher). An understanding of writing apprehension is particularly helpful when teachers deal with students who have trouble producing drafts—their difficulty might be anxiety rather than laziness or inattention. We can help such students learn conscious coping strategies, such as using their anxiety as a cue to stay on task and to verbalize strategies (Meichenbaum and Butler), as Will had learned to do.

As the psychological community began to focus on the importance of mental events, a more cognitive view of achievement motivation developed—attribution theory. This theory, put forward in its fullest form by Weiner in *An*

Attributional Theory of Motivation and Emotion, examines causal attributions, that is, people's beliefs about the reasons for the outcomes of their efforts. Particularly important for motivation is the perception of what Rotter calls the "locus of control"—whether individuals believe that success or failure in an achievement situation is a result of internal forces (ability) or of external forces (task difficulty). We can classify people along a continuum from internal to external according to their beliefs about causality (another way of looking at deCharms's origins and pawns). Thus we can have two different reactions to the same phenomenon: some students tell us that they don't understand an assignment, assuming the cause is internal, while others tell us the assignment is too hard, assuming the cause is external. Attribution theory also looks at beliefs about the causes of outcomes along the dimensions of stability (aptitude) and instability (chance), and controllability (effort) and uncontrollability (fatigue). Thus we have students who take credit for their success or failure themselves, while others tell us they were just lucky, or that their grandmother died.

The notion underlying attribution theory—that people's beliefs about the outcomes of achievement situations guide their behavior in those situations—also formed the basis for research on learned helplessness. Researchers found that when a dog was put in a shock-avoidance experiment but could do nothing to avoid the shocks, the animal later did nothing to avoid shocks in a later experiment where escape was available (Seligman and Maier). The dog had learned an existential lesson, that it could exercise no control over events in its world. The result was helpless, hopeless passivity.

Researchers examining this phenomenon in humans (Diener and Dweck; Dweck and Goetz) have looked at patterns of attributions—characteristic ways of explaining failure or success—and have named two such patterns: an adaptive, persistent mastery orientation and a maladaptive pattern of learned helplessness. When put in a situation where they first achieved success in solving problems and then encountered insoluble problems, mastery-oriented students like An Mei did not attribute their failure to their own inadequacies but began to search for new strategies and to give themselves instructions on how to proceed. Their prognosis for future success remained positive, as did their affective state; a number indicated heightened affect in the face of a challenging opportunity for mastery. They either maintained or improved their problem-solving strategies, and many showed more sophisticated strategies during the failure experience than they had shown earlier in the success situation. They persisted in the face of failure because they seemed to see it as an opportunity for new learning.[4] The helpless students, on the other hand, displayed a behavioral pattern that contrasted with that of the mastery-oriented students in every way. When they encountered failure, they attributed it to their own lack of ability. They had negative expectations for their future performance at problem-solving, and a significant number believed that if they were given the problems they had solved in the first part of the experiment, they could no longer solve them. As they continued to encounter failure, their affective state became more negative, and they slipped into more unsophisticated and unproductive problem-solving strategies; even their recall of their previous successes declined—they remembered more failures than they actually had during the first part of the experiment. They saw failure not as a challenge but as a measure of their ability, a defeat (Dweck and Bempechat).

One of the researchers' most interesting findings was that there appear to be significant sex differences in learned helplessness. Although females are generally more successful than males in school, especially in verbal skills (see Rubin and Greene), they are more likely than males to attribute their successes to outside factors and their failures to lack of ability. They are more likely to give up than to persist if they fail. Males, on the other hand, are more likely to attribute their successes to their own abilities and their failures to outside factors[5]; they tend to persist and even improve in the face of failure. The way our culture socializes boys and girls has been blamed for these attributional differences (see Dweck and Goetz for a summary of this research); whatever the cause, it is important for teachers to understand that for students like An Mei with a mastery orientation, failure may be a spur, while for others like Ira it may produce passivity and encourage their view that trying to improve is hopeless. We can help alleviate learned helplessness by teaching students specific strategies (such as breaking a large task into smaller parts), guiding them through the writing process, and assuring them that they won't be penalized for errors during the process. We can also help students analyze their goals and judge their own competence realistically. One way to do this is through a discussion of goals in an achievement setting, contrasting learning goals with performance goals.

Analyzing Achievement Goals: A Social-Cognitive Perspective

Examining patterns of attribution helps us understand why people *expect* to succeed; but why do they *want* to succeed? Dweck and Elliott and Elliott and Dweck propose that people in achievement situations can set two classes of goals: learning goals, which aim to increase competence, or performance goals, which aim to gain favorable judgments of competence (or to avoid being judged as incompetent). Each class of goals can be traced to a tacit theory of intelligence. Some students subscribe to a theory of intelligence as incremental, as something they can increase through their own effort.[6] Therefore, when confronted with a challenging task, they believe they can do it and are interested in learning something from it. They see errors as ways to learn and effort as an investment in that learning. Other students subscribe to a theory of intelligence as a stable entity, something that cannot be changed through effort—indeed, effort is risky because it might result in error and reveal inadequacy. When confronted with a challenging task, they do not ask, "How can I do it?" but, *"Can* I do it?" They are more oriented toward being judged as smart than toward learning something new. Although the two theories of intelligence are unrelated to ability in young children, over time the theories begin to predict achievement—entity theorists wind up as low achievers and incremental theorists as high achievers (Dweck and Bempechat). A table developed by Dweck and Elliott points out the contrasts between the two theories of intelligence and the related classes of achievement goals (see below).

While both classes of goals are natural and inevitable ones in achievement situations, Elliott and Dweck found that an overemphasis on performance goals not only helped to create learned helplessness in some students, but it also had an effect on mastery-oriented students, making them so protective of how their ability would be judged that they later rejected the chance to learn something new if it involved risking errors. So while students' theories of intelligence may orient them toward either learning or performance goals, situational cues in the classroom environment can do much to help construct—or deconstruct—their goal orientations and build their theories of intelligence. The notion of "giftedness," emphasized in many public schools through tracking systems, contributes heavily to students' theories of intelligence. Palmquist and Young found that belief in the notion of giftedness (that is, writing ability is a stable entity that one is born with, something like perfect pitch) played a significant role in shaping students' expectations. Students with low assessments of their writing ability had both strong beliefs in giftedness and high levels of writing apprehension, while students with high estimates of their writing ability had a low belief in giftedness (they were, in other words, incremental theorists) and showed low writing apprehension.

What happens when students set achievement goals, like Will's goal for improving an already excellent paper?

Table 1. Students' Theories of Intelligence and Achievement Goals

Theories of Intelligence

	Incremental	Entity
Intelligence is:	A repertoire of skills that increases through effort	A global, stable entity whose adequacy is judged through performance
Effort is:	An investment that increases intelligence	A risk that may reveal low intelligence

Goals

	Learning Goal: Competence Increase	Performance Goal: Competence Judgment
1. Entering question:	How can I do it? What will I learn?	Can I do it? Will I look smart?
2. Focus on:	Process	Outcome
3. Errors:	Natural, useful	Failure
4. Uncertainty:	Challenging	Threatening
5. Optimal task:	Maximizes learning (becoming smarter)	Maximizes looking smart
6. Seek:	Accurate information about ability	Flattering information
7. Standards:	Personal, long-term, flexible	Normative, immediate, rigid
8. Expectancy:	Emphasizes effort	Emphasizes present ability
9. Teacher:	Resource, guide	Judge, rewarder/punisher
10. Goal value:	"Intrinsic": value of skill, activity, progress	"Extrinsic": value of judgment

Source: Adapted from Carol Dweck and Elaine S. Elliott, "Achievement Motivation," *Handbook of Child Psychology*, ed. Paul H. Mussen and E. Mavis Hetherington, vol. 4 (New York: Wiley, 1983) 655. Reprinted by permission of John Wiley & Sons, Inc.

Dweck theorizes that students enter such a situation with a repertoire of cognitive and motivational sets. Cognitive sets include the theories of intelligence (incremental or entity) mentioned above. Motivational sets include beliefs (views about the nature of competence, the level of one's own competence, about what variables influence outcomes, and so on), inference rules (preferred modes of estimating task difficulty, deciding the causes of outcomes), salient representations (tendencies to focus on the pleasant or unpleasant means or desirable or undesirable outcomes), and values and interests (personal hierarchies of what is important and enjoyable). Situational cues about the evaluator, the nature of the task, and the possible rewards are then interpreted in light of these motivational sets. Students set goals, have some expectancy about achieving those goals, and have some idea about how pleasant or unpleasant the means to achievement will be. They then set a course of action that when completed will feed back into the system, potentially altering their goal values, expectancies, or means values. Students will persist in trying to achieve the goals they have set as long as their values and expectancies remain high ("Motivation" 92–93). An examination of these values and expectancies can help us understand our students' achievement behavior more completely.

Goal Values and Goal Expectancies (Confidence)

As mentioned earlier, we can differentiate between two classes of goals in terms of values: learning goals and performance goals. Students (like An Mei) who set learning goals aim at increasing their competence, at understanding the material, or mastering a task. Students (like Alice) who set performance goals aim at validating their competence, at getting favorable judgments of their ability, and avoiding unfavorable judgments. While students seem disposed toward one learning framework or the other, Dweck points out that adopting one or the other set of goals in the classroom has specific effects on students' motivation and on their subsequent achievement behavior with regard to their standards for achievement, perceived control, task choice, task interest, task pursuit, outcome attribution, and satisfaction with the task ("Motivation" 99–102). Let us examine each of these more closely.

"Standards" refers to the level of performance a student must achieve in order to feel successful. Learning goals appear to foster personal standards for success, ones that are flexible and progressive, allowing students to mark their own progress and maintain interest, even in the face of failure. Performance goals, on the other hand, appear to encourage the adoption of normative standards—comparing one's progress to those of other students. Such standards can create a "win-lose" situation where considerable personal progress can be negated by comparative evaluation (Ames and Ames). Students presented with learning goals need not worry about the abilities of others when confronting a challenging task; they need to think only about how much effort they expect to put forth, given the task and their perceptions of their ability. But students presented with performance goals will first estimate their ability in relation to others'; if the estimate is high, they will proceed, but if they have doubts about their ability, they will avoid challenge. A competitive classroom atmosphere can therefore be detrimental to student motivation. Perceived control, as mentioned earlier, is an important factor in determining motivation. Students in a classroom with learning goals have more control over the factors that relate to attaining those goals; they set their own standard for success, they use peers and teachers as resources rather than as potential obstacles, and they evaluate their own progress. Students who are given performance goals have less control over outcomes, since they perceive that others are judging their success or failure against normative criteria rather than against their personal progress.

Task choice, task interest, and task pursuit also show

how having learning or performance goals can influence student behavior. A classroom that sets learning goals encourages students to choose more challenging tasks, regardless of their perceived ability; one that sets only performance goals encourages students with low expectancies to choose easy tasks to ensure success and to avoid negative judgments of their abilities. Learning goals appear to promote interest in the task itself and to create positive rather than negative affective responses in the face of difficulties. Performance goals foster interest in the judgment of one's ability and negative responses when it appears that ability is in question. With learning goals, high effort is more likely to be experienced as pleasurable, nurturing a sense of pride in achievement, whereas with performance goals, effort is seen as evidence of low ability, fostering a sense of shame. Learning goals help students persist in the face of challenge, while performance goals lead students to pursue tasks in ineffective ways, to engage in face-saving behavior (for example, to minimize effort and then use that as an excuse for poor performance),[7] or to avoid challenging tasks altogether.

Finally, the two goal frameworks produce different behaviors in terms of outcome attribution and satisfaction. In a learning framework, both success and failure are attributed to effort, and students' satisfaction with their labor is related to the degree of effort put forth; in the face of difficulties, students do not attribute outcomes to lack of ability. In a performance framework, students see success and failure as a reflection of their ability and luck; their satisfaction is related to the degree of ability and luck they think they have. Clearly, a learning framework is more desirable than a performance framework in terms of goal values.

Now let us look at goal expectancies, students' confidence in their ability to attain learning and performance goals. Expectancies have a lot to do with confidence; one would expect that students who have done well in school and on standardized tests (and who therefore have ample evidence of their abilities) to be the most confident in their expectancies for future success, while only failure-prone students would have shaky confidence and low expectancies for future achievement. But this is not the case. Some low achievers have high confidence, attributing their difficulties to outside factors rather than to their own ability. A recent study found an entire class full of basic writers who had higher self-esteem and lower writing apprehension than the 16 classes of regular freshman composition in the study (Minot and Gamble). Some high-achievers have very fragile confidence; they attribute their failures to a lack of ability, and they have low expectancies for their ability to take on challenging tasks in the future. Studies have found that this tendency among high achievers to have low confidence is especially prevalent among bright females (Dweck, "Motivation" 108).

Research has found that establishing and maintaining appropriately high expectancies for success are fostered by the tendency to focus on strategy, on progress, and on past and future success (Dweck, "Motivation" 110; see Dweck and Elliott for a more detailed analysis of expectancy formation). When approaching a task, students who can strategize and can keep thinking about strategy when difficulties arise learn to expect that they will be successful at completing the task, but students who analyze the task only in terms of its difficulty and their chances of success learn to have low expectancies. Students who adopt challenging standards based on personal progress, who remind themselves of that progress, and who focus on effort and strategy as the means by which they make progress will form expectancies of success and have confidence in their abilities. In contrast, students who focus on normative standards as a measure of their own success and focus on ability rather than effort and strategy will form low expectancies of success. The research of Belenky, Clinchy, Goldberger, and Tarule on women's ways of knowing may explain why so many female students have low confidence in spite of their academic success. Belenky and her colleagues postulate that many women are "connected knowers"—that is, they focus on trying to understand the perspective and reality of others as they learn. A corollary of this notion is that women are socialized more than men to be aware of and responsive to the opinions of others; therefore it is more difficult for women to establish autonomy in setting goals and in focusing on their own progress without attending to how others are doing. Furthermore, the very success of some low-confidence students appears to undermine what confidence they have; if they see high ability as something that makes tasks easy, answers obvious, and effort unnecessary, then past success is evidence only that they have succeeded at easier tasks (Dweck, "Motivation" 117). Expending a good deal of effort and strategizing is evidence to them not of an intelligent approach to problem-solving but of a lack of ability. If they were just smart enough, they wouldn't have to work so hard.

Motivation in the Writing Classroom

Given this research, what is the best way for writing teachers to help motivate students who need it and to keep motivated students energized? First, it seems clear what not to do—to try to increase student confidence by giving short, easy tasks that assure error-free success and by lavishing large amounts of praise. The research tells us that such an approach will not encourage students to seek longer, more challenging tasks, promote persistence in the face of failure, or help them persevere when immediate rewards are not present. (This counterproductive approach—giving easy tasks to establish a pattern of errorless learning—is, alas, often used with the best of intentions in the basic writing curriculum. See Rose, "Remedial.") Instead, we need to think about how to help students understand and make good use of motivational processes, and how to create a classroom environment that promotes learning goals rather than performance goals.

First of all, we can use teaching strategies that research

has proven effective: we can make theories of intelligence explicit to our students, ask them to monitor their motivational as well as their cognitive and affective processes, and discuss strategies for persisting, progressing, and succeeding at challenging tasks. We can give explicit instruction to students in motivational strategies (as deCharms did with his origins and pawns). We can instruct students to take challenge or failure as a cue to increase effort (as Dweck did with children who exhibited "helpless" behavior; see "Role"). We can teach them, as Meichenbaum and Butler did, to also use their affective states as cues to spur them on rather than as evidence that they aren't able to do the task. We can instruct them not only in these cognitive and affective strategies but also in why the strategies are important, since as Paris points out, students who learn new strategies without also learning appropriate metacognitive strategies—knowing *when* as well as *how* to proceed—will not use the new strategies appropriately. And we need to remember that it is not just the low achievers who might need help understanding their goals and attributions, since high achievers can also have motivational sets that need attention. We can present students with the frameworks of learning and performance goals and discuss the fact that the writing classroom focuses on learning goals. Then we have to make that promise good.

A glance back at Table 1 shows that the environment of the process-oriented writing classroom is already in many ways one that fosters learning goals. We are, as Elbow (*Embracing Contraries*) and others remind us, coaches as well as judges, resources and guides for our students as well as evaluators of their work. We do not focus on error but look at error as a window into the student's thinking and writing process. We expect that all students can learn to write, that they can increase their skill through effort. Still, we can do more. Since all motivational research tells us that perceived control is such an important issue, we can establish frameworks within which the student takes control of certain things—task choice, for example. We can establish evaluation procedures in which students have some say (for example, self-evaluations, peer evaluations, choices over which pieces go into a portfolio or when pieces are ready to be evaluated). We can publish student writing (in a class magazine), including not just the best pieces in terms of normative standards but also the best piece from each student. We can establish teacher-researcher projects where we involve students in research on their own learning; as Goswami and Stillman point out, such research provides students with a good deal of intrinsic motivation for discussion, reading, and writing. We can establish cooperative learning projects (such as a class newsletter with a rotating editor) that aim at motivating students by having them take responsibility for the learning of others as well as for themselves.[8] We can, in short, provide both the cognitive framework and the social situation for students to enhance their own motivational skills. It is not that we simply need to stimulate students' enjoyment of learning, as Csikszentmihalyi suggests in the epigraph to this chapter; but enjoyment is certainly a by-product of achievement behavior motivated by learning goals. Our classrooms will be more enjoyable places for ourselves as well as for our students if we can focus on such goals.

☜ 4 ☞

Beliefs and Attitudes

The real meaning of a liberal education goes far
beyond just teaching the student how to be a doctor, a
lawyer, a diplomat, or a business executive. A liberal
education is really about encouraging the student to
grapple with some of life's most fundamental
questions.
—Alexander Astin, *What Matters in College?*

We are past the halfway mark in the semester. Students
have started the library paper, an assignment that asks them
to integrate the reading and discussions in class with some
library research. The assignment is not long enough to be a
full-dress "research paper," but it does require them to summarize, paraphrase, and quote references. It also requires
the objective stance of academic prose and the use of evidence to support a thesis.

Their reading assignments have focused on the world
of Islam: a piece on early Islamic science, another on the art
of calligraphy, one explaining the Five Pillars of Islam, a few
selections from the Quran, and a piece on the Nation of Islam in the United States. I also have brought in several news
articles on events in the Middle East, trying through a discussion of these events to help students separate out the religion of Islam itself from some of its radical political
manifestations. The class discussion indicates to me that the
tenets of this religion, as familiar as some of them may seem,

are still pretty foreign to the students. Islam and its believers are not a noticeable presence in the Pacific Northwest; I
am afraid my students are using the popular media stereotype of "Arab" as a filter for the readings. On campus we
have a small mosque, organized and run by a group of international students and faculty. I call and ask if they could
send a speaker, to give these ideas a local habitation and a
name. I am expecting a man (which says something about
my own stereotypes). The speaker turns out to be a young
woman, a local resident who has converted to Islam. She
comes to class wearing a dun-colored robe and a sort of
wimple, a costume she has fashioned herself derived from
her study of the Quran. It covers her entirely except for her
face, making me think of the nuns of my childhood. The
students are visibly uneasy watching and listening to this
apple-cheeked ex-Lutheran. She is, I think to myself, the Self
who has become the Other, a visible and vocal challenge to
their beliefs, attitudes, and values. During the question and
answer session, Ed, who saw action in the Middle East when
he was in the army, pushes her about the status of women in
Islam; she answers by quoting the Prophet. Other questions
are answered in a similar way. The students are polite but
dissatisfied with her answers. It is one of the most spirited
class sessions yet—even Tom has his head up off his desk
and is paying attention.

Three students are having difficulty dealing with the
very subject matter of Islam. After class Alberto tells me that
he needs to talk to me. I have asked the class to summarize
the reading on the Five Pillars, to make sure they understand
the basic tenets of the religion and also to help them with
techniques for summarization as they get ready to write the
library paper. He is visibly agitated, perhaps in part because
of the speaker and her firm insistence on the superiority of
her religion. "I can't write this," he tells me, jabbing at the
assignment sheet with his forefinger and getting red in the
face. "I don't believe it!" Alberto belongs to a pre-Vatican II
Catholic congregation, a breakaway group that was just pub-

licly condemned by the local bishop. In a conference the week before, he told me he was dropping his biological sciences class because the teacher "kept talking about Darwinism," a theory Alberto doesn't agree with. He must be feeling under siege from all sides. Trying to be soothing, I tell him that I didn't expect people to believe everything they read or heard—that in fact I hoped they wouldn't, citing a few Elvis/aliens tabloid headlines I have seen recently in the supermarket. I go on (a bit too long) about how he would be reading and discussing many ideas that he didn't agree with and that one of the purposes of college is to encounter other beliefs and values in order to sort out one's own. All I want to do is help him understand how to summarize and also to understand people like the speaker a bit better. He leaves, still not happy about the assignment. My little sermon on critical thinking and tolerance doesn't help much; his "summary" turns out to be a rather disjointed refutation of the Five Pillars, at the end of which he has written, "I can't write about things that offend me." How can I help him deal with and write about ideas like these that challenge his beliefs?

Heather is also having trouble. She is active in the campus Youth for Christ group and spends most of her social time with friends from that organization. Nothing in her experience, either in her campus activities or in her rural background, has prepared her for confronting ideas so foreign to her beliefs. She did an acceptable summary of the Five Pillars, but now she wants to write a library paper that compares Islam and Christianity. I am nervous about this topic, knowing (in part from my experience with Alberto) the kind of polemic it could produce, and try to steer her toward a more neutral topic—Islamic art, perhaps; but she tells me that this is the first time she is writing about something she really cares about. How can I deny this earnest young woman? The first draft turns out to be an impassioned piece on the evils of Islam compared to the true path to God, a piece that assumes an audience of fellow believers. I want to approach the revision delicately, so as not to offend her deeply held beliefs, but I am concerned about the final portfolio readings. If she puts this paper in the portfolio, I know it will come back with a low ranking and the comment "this is not research-based." (Even though we tend toward sermonizing ourselves, as I did with Alberto, academics are fairly intolerant of student sermons.)[1] One important quality of academic writing is "the giving of reasons and evidence rather than just opinions, feelings, experiences" (Elbow, "Reflections" 140). How can I move her away from a polemic to a more reasoned and reasonable piece?

Then there is Jaymie. She is less intense in her reaction to the speaker and the assignment (the two have become intertwined in all three of these students' minds), but she is also clearly troubled. She talks with me about what she describes as "confusion": being committed to her own religious beliefs and not knowing how to deal with a paper about Islam in an academic (that is, objective) way. We talk a bit about how one can be committed to beliefs and still be tolerant of other ways of believing and thinking about the world. She chooses the same topic as Heather—a comparison of Islam and her own faith—and through much effort on her part the result is not a polemic; it is, however, a bit like the genre I think of as the "high school report." How can I help her come up with a thesis for this piece while at the same time not do harm to the thoughtful, objective tone she has worked so hard to achieve?

The Challenge to/of Beliefs and Attitudes

As universities move toward accepting—indeed, actively promoting—diversity on campus and in the curriculum, scenes like these are being played out in other classrooms as well. The difficulties our students have with issues of cultural difference stem in part from the K–12 classrooms they come from, where such ideas are often seen as controversial. As Oliver documents in her book on multiculturalism, censorship is a growing problem for the public schools (39–52). In the past two decades, the religious right has been growing steadily in size and sophistication. Conservative groups have organized themselves in various ways to deal with what they consider dangerously liberal ideas.[2] Some activists have visited school classes and libraries searching for "un-American" books—often those having to do with the experience of Jews, women, African Americans, or Hispanics. In one case in New York, a list of "mentally dangerous" works included authors Bernard Malamud, Richard Wright, Kurt Vonnegut, and Langston Hughes (Moffett, *Storm* 29). Conservative Christian groups in Yucaipa, California, brought about the removal of a whole-language textbook series ("Impressions") because in their eyes some of the selections challenged traditional family values. One of the objectionable stories was "Beauty and the Beast." Another quoted the traditional rhyme "Lavender's Blue," which has the line "And we shall be gay, dilly dilly, and we shall both dance"; since two little boys in the story had earlier exchanged valentines, some parents saw the text as endorsing homosexuality (Meade 40). One result of this pressure from the right, as Moffett's *Storm in the Mountains* shows, is that publishers selling language arts textbook series have in effect censored themselves, cutting anything that might be considered even remotely controversial. Books that do arouse controversy, like Moffett's "Interaction" series, are dropped.

The effects of these challenges should not be underestimated. The publishing industry, dominated by large corporations, is naturally more interested in profit margins than controversy over texts.[3] Once purchased by schools, the safe vanilla textbooks these publishers produce remain in use for some time. K–12 teachers who have encountered resistance to new ideas from a group of impassioned parents may be excused if they shy away from the issues that produced such passion, or a pedagogy that aims at helping students think for themselves; teachers in the Yucaipa case have received harassing phone calls and physical threats (Meade 37–38).

Hence, many students today come to higher education from classroom environments and curricula that have consciously avoided all issues that might be construed as controversial. One of the first university classes they encounter is a writing course that encourages critical thinking and often requires reading about issues they may have been told should not be discussed in school. No wonder students are unprepared for the kinds of ideas we discuss and the way we discuss them in college. No wonder some of them are put off, feeling their valued beliefs are threatened.

The English 101 curriculum at my institution is part of our new general education core of courses for entering students, involving readings from world cultures. At the heart of this curriculum is a conscious effort to promote tolerance, to help students understand what it means to live in a world and a nation made up of different cultures and ideologies. But of course it is not enough to simply introduce students to other cultures and ways of doing and believing; they will sometimes react as Alberto did by rejecting out of hand anything that seems "other," because it offends them. I try to practice a pedagogy that affirms the individual student but also works to promote tolerance of difference and to challenge outright misconceptions about race, ethnicity, and gender (see Whitten; Adams). While I am respectful of my students' religious beliefs, I am also aware of the research that shows a link between religious fundamentalism and discriminatory attitudes (Allport, *Nature*; Kirkpatrick).[4] I want my students to develop a more skeptical habit of mind, one that questions assumptions, looks for evidence, and does not blindly accept authority as always right. I agree with Bizzell ("Politics") and Stotsky that teaching cannot be value-neutral; recent examples of ethnic violence give a special urgency to my thinking about diversity and cultural pluralism in the classroom, to my commitment to the kind of ethical community I want not only in my classroom but also in society. I do not want to tell my students *what* to think, but I do want to teach them *how* to think for themselves.[5] This is the value of a liberal arts education—the *artes liberales* that in a Roman education were those subjects and skills necessary for the development of a free man, a citizen. When we challenge our students' deeply held beliefs and attitudes by discussing difference, we are not trying to change their beliefs to agree with ours; we are merely trying to help them understand that there are other ways of believing that other people hold just as deeply. We are, in other words, trying to move them toward more open-minded stances as they grapple with (in Astin's words) the fundamental questions of life. In order to manage such a challenge effectively, teachers need to know about the nature of beliefs and belief systems.

What Are Beliefs and Attitudes?

There is little consensus in the academic community about the definition of "belief." Bar-Tal identifies beliefs as units of knowledge, including within this broad definition such notions as hypotheses, inferences, values, intentions, and ideologies. According to Bar-Tal, knowledge encompasses all the beliefs one accumulates through any means, scientific or otherwise—facts as well as faith (5). Rokeach (*Beliefs*) and Fishbein and Ajzen, the most well known social scientists who have written about the phenomenon, agree that belief is cognition; in the field of composition we are familiar with this notion thanks to the social constructionists, who identify knowledge as socially justified belief (see Bruffee, "Social"). The view of beliefs proposed by the philosophers (and used by most of us in ordinary parlance) differentiates between knowledge and belief (Griffiths). Knowledge is seen as justified true belief, while other kinds of knowledge (not justified) involve subjective states of mind about propositions. People *know* that if they drop something, it will fall down rather than up, and that during the winter it is cold in this part of the country. People *believe* that a particular race or religion is superior (or inferior), that cultural pluralism and tolerance are central (or not) to the survival of democracy in America, that there is (or is not) a supreme being in charge of the universe.

However they may disagree on the definition, most who write about beliefs do agree that beliefs are propositions or statements of relations among things that are accepted as true. Beliefs underlie attitude formation (Fishbein and Ajzen; Rokeach, *Beliefs*); an attitude is a predisposition to action, a readiness to respond in certain ways. To accept a proposition as true is to invest it with some value. Some people feel deeply enough about their most cherished beliefs to die or to kill for them. It is this class of beliefs and attitudes—those that are heavily value-laden and therefore charged with affect—that I would like to examine in this chapter; these are usually, but not exclusively, religious and/or political beliefs. Because they carry affective freight, value-laden beliefs can give rise to the emotions that either facilitate or interfere with students' writing processes, as discussed in chapter 2. As teachers, we need to know more about how our students' beliefs and attitudes are formed and how we can help students understand them as they interact with their writing processes.

Psychological and Social Theories

As with emotions, beliefs and attitudes can be examined from two different but related points of view: the psychological or individual, and the social or contextual. The former attempts to explain the mental phenomenon of belief formation and the relation between beliefs and attitudes; the latter looks at belief systems and their maintenance, especially in groups of believers.

Fishbein and Ajzen, whose attitude-behavior theory is the standard reference for research on beliefs, propose an information-processing model for belief formation (131–34). Beliefs may arise in one of three ways: from experiences with an object (descriptive belief), from inferences made based on some other belief (inferential belief), and from other sources of information (informational belief). Beliefs about an object lead to an attitude toward it, which in turn leads toward behavioral intentions (for example, good, therefore seek out, or bad, therefore avoid). These intentions affect the actual behaviors toward an object. Behaviors then feed back to beliefs, either reinforcing or modifying them, depending on the results of the behavior toward the object. If the results of behavior toward an object reinforce the belief, the attitudes about the object will be strengthened. If, on the other hand, the experience with the object is not reinforced, the beliefs may change (positively or negatively), and the resulting attitudes will change as well.

Here is how the process works. My own beliefs about the timber industry (the object) have been influenced largely by my encounters with ugly clear-cuts in this part of the country (my experience with the object), my inferences about the industry based on what I know about other industries having to do with natural resources (like oil), and my reading and conversations, especially conversations with a colleague who is an ecofeminist. (I suspect my undergraduate study of romantic poetry also had an influence on my beliefs about and attitudes toward nature.) Until recently, I believed the timber industry to be male-dominated, embodying the Western ethic of dominion over nature rather than living in harmony with it. My attitudes toward the industry were negative. These beliefs and attitudes influenced my verbal behavior when I discussed issues of the environment.

This year, however, I have had occasion to discuss issues of environmental education with representatives from a large timber company, one that has reforested the Mt. St. Helens blast area. These representatives included a forest research hydrologist, a former teacher turned corporate executive, and a forester with experience in forest management, forest research, and science education in the United States and overseas. They immediately challenged my stereotype of the industry, in part because of their education and background, in part because all three are women. My behavioral intention when I first met with them was to listen and to be open-minded, but I was not convinced that I had any attitudes about the subject that should change. In one particularly interesting session over dinner, I found that these representatives shared many of my attitudes and beliefs about the environment, that in spite of different viewpoints we shared some important values. My contact with these three thoughtful and articulate women, from whom I have learned a good deal, has challenged my beliefs about the timber industry (or at least about this company as a member of that industry), which in turn has changed my negative attitudes and my verbal behavior in conversations with my colleagues about environmental issues.

Belief Systems

Beliefs and their accompanying attitudes do not exist in isolation from one another; they are part of systems that are organized in a way that makes sense psychologically if not logically (Rokeach, *Beliefs* 2). The size of the belief system and the degree of interrelatedness of beliefs within the system can vary from domain to domain—a person's religious beliefs may be very organized, while his or her beliefs about the effects of living near a nuclear power plant might be organized or not, depending on the proximity of such a plant. All belief systems have certain characteristics in common (Borhek and Curtis 9–16). Along with the actual content of the system comes a set of values; these values define what is right and wrong for the believer. The system also has some set criteria for establishing those values (the word of God or of Marx and Lenin, for example). There is an implicit logic to the system, although that logic is not always consistently applied (it is easy to promise to love your neighbor in the abstract, but it might be harder in actuality, depending on your neighbors). The system also provides a perspective, a cognitive map for believers to position themselves with regard to other things, especially other groups and world views (the "other" is the infidel or an equal). The system comes with a set of prescriptions and proscriptions (action alternatives or policy recommendations—thou shalt/ thou shalt not) and a technology (that is, an accepted means to attain valued goals—prayer, protest marches). A belief system might be idiosyncratic (as in the case of a person who believes he is Napoleon), or it might be shared with large numbers of other persons (as in the case of religious groups or political parties). Most importantly, for our purposes in the writing classroom, a system might be "open" in the sense that its structure allows for change and acceptance of new ideas, or it might be "closed," rejecting any ideas that do not conform to the system and intolerant of all but those with similar beliefs; the closed belief system relies heavily on the word of authorities for its maintenance (Rokeach, *Open*).

Understanding the difference between the closed and the open system will help teachers better understand students like Alberto, Heather, and Jaymie. All belief systems serve two powerful but conflicting sets of motives: the need for a cognitive framework to make sense of the world and the need to ward off threatening aspects of reality. When the cognitive need to know is predominant and the need to ward off threat is low or absent, the system is open; for those holding open belief systems, the world is seen as a relatively friendly place; in the open system the power of authority is not absent, but that power depends on the authority's consistency with other information about the world. Authorities who give information in conflict with the belief system will be considered unreliable.

But in the closed belief system, the need to ward off threat is stronger than the cognitive need to know (Rokeach, *Open* 67–68), as in the case of conservative groups in the censorship cases mentioned earlier—or as in the case of Alberto, who could not summarize ideas that were in conflict with his beliefs. The more closed the system, the greater the belief in the rightness and power of authority. Those outside the closed system are evaluated according to the authorities they line themselves up with; closed system believers have difficulty separating out and evaluating beliefs from the person who holds them (62–63), as my three students who couldn't talk about Islam without talking too about the class speaker. The more closed the system, the more different ideas and people threaten it. Those who hold closed belief systems, like Alberto (and like the conservative groups demanding censorship of ideas in the public schools), feel anxious and threatened much of the time.

The social aspect of shared belief systems is extremely powerful. People strive to hold "correct" beliefs about the world, and when objective evidence is not available to them, they will test the accuracy of their beliefs and attitudes by comparing them with the beliefs and attitudes of others (Festinger, "Social"). This social aspect of belief systems is one reason that religious groups like the Amish (who adhere to a closed system) forbid contact with the world outside the one they have created for themselves; that contact would interfere with the continuance of the system as it is now constituted. Yet personal commitment is one of the most salient features of many belief systems (Borhek and Curtis 6). The conflict between that commitment and the need to test the accuracy of one's beliefs by comparing them with those of others produces some of the stress of the first year of college. Students like Alberto, Heather, and Jaymie adhere to belief systems that rely heavily on authority; they come to the university from environments in which they were surrounded by other people very much like themselves who gave them feedback that reinforced their closed systems. Now they find themselves encountering conflicting authorities, encountering people and ideas unlike theirs; their beliefs are challenged rather than reinforced by some of their social experience. The emotion aroused as a result of this experience (in George Mandler's terms, an interruption of expectations) may be expressed variously—anger in Alberto's case, confusion in Jaymie's—but if it is intense enough, it can interfere with their thinking and writing processes.

The Cultural and Organizational Contexts of Belief Systems

The culture of the university itself challenges student belief systems. Culture consists in large part of learned and shared ideas; belief systems are part of a culture, instances of it, and have social consequences. A shared belief system having to do with the superiority of the Aryan race allowed the Holocaust to occur. In a more mundane instance, the culture that values individual achievement in the humanities (especially in America, where individualism is highly valued) leads to suspicion of collaborative research and writing—the reason our students at first resist writing groups, our academic colleagues don't understand collaborative classrooms, and our coauthored publications are questioned in tenure and promotion reviews (see Ede and Lunsford ix–x).

Shared belief systems and their accompanying attitudes are carried and perpetuated by social structures and associations. These structures can be relatively unspecialized (like a kinship structure or a neighborhood), or they can be associations and organizations formed for some specific purpose, which may (as in the case of a church) or may not (as in the case of a corporation) be the belief system itself. All associations have belief systems with certain characteristics, for example, a corporate body, a membership, or a larger community of believers. Those that have become fairly institutionalized tend to expand beyond the original purpose for the association, have members for which the association is a career and develop hierarchies for those careers, and have connections with other associations of like kinds. They also have a shared discourse. The belief system provides a context in which otherwise cryptic messages ("power to the people," "family values") can be understood, since the rest is implicit for those who share the beliefs (Borhek and Curtis 60–79).

The university is an example of an association that carries a belief system. Every institution of higher education has a mission statement, articulating what the members of the association are to believe and value. Unlike churches, colleges and universities are not organized for the purpose of the belief system; academic believers focus not on the content of the shared belief system but on the process—the process of open inquiry in the pursuit of knowledge, of understanding, perhaps even of wisdom. One important part of the belief system of universities is open-mindedness in the pursuit of new knowledge or in classroom discussion; an old academic saw has it that the only thing professors will not tolerate is ignorance. Of course, we all know that academics can be as dogmatic as the next believer, holding a particular belief system (radical constructivism, Marxism, behaviorism) and defending it at all costs; but the fact remains that one of our most cherished beliefs is in the sanctity of academic freedom—a belief that includes not only our own right to be free from interference with what we teach and research but also a respect for the rights of others in the free interchange of ideas. When we teach our students the value of an open, inquiring mind as a major component of a liberal education, we are conveying a central aspect of our belief system.

Our shared discourse, academic prose, has characteristics that reflect our shared belief system: this specialized discourse sets out a position or proposition, weighs and marshals evidence to support the position, and invokes the work and positions of others. Academic prose is by no means passionless, but unlike the polemics our students are used to in other arenas, our discourse acknowledges the fact that other ways of thinking about an issue exist. As Elbow says, "[M]ost academics reflect in their writing and teaching a belief that passionate commitment is permissible, even desirable—so long as it is balanced by awareness that it is a passionate position, what the stakes are, how others might argue otherwise" ("Reflections" 142). Students used to associations that carry belief systems with different rules for discourse get into difficulty when attempting academic prose; witness Alberto, who on the works cited page of his library paper listed the author of the Bible as "God."

From Closed to Open Belief Systems

The writing process is also a thinking process. Students with closed belief systems of any sort have learned to accept authority (a particular authority) and not to weigh evidence, test ideas, think critically. When we talk about student beliefs and attitudes that keep them from engaging in such critical thinking, we are in fact invoking models of intellectual and ethical development—those of Perry and of Belenky, Clinchy, Goldberger, and Tarule. We want to move our students away from thinking that authorities have all the answers, an early stage of thinking these theorists describe, toward what we as academics think of as more "mature" thinking—a commitment to particular beliefs while acknowledging the existence of belief systems that are equally valid for others.

How might we work to bring about such a change? A common assumption is that interpersonal contact with those who are different will establish more open ways of looking at difference (this is the assumption behind such phenomena as the Goodwill Games or student exchange programs). But mere contact is not enough; sometimes such contact can reinforce negative beliefs (as when the speaker from the mosque came to my class). Because people test the accuracy of their beliefs by comparing them to the beliefs and attitudes of others, active participation rather than just contact with those who think differently can help bring about change in the way students think about issues. Through focused, positive social interaction, students can test their beliefs against the beliefs of others and modify their way of believing accordingly. Astin, in his study of the impact of a college education, finds that the single most important environmental influence on student development is the peer group; "by judicious and imaginative use of peer groups, any college or university can substantially strengthen its impact on student learning and personal development" (xiv). When writing groups give suggestions for revision, they are also suggesting a revision of thinking.

Assignments that focus on the development of empathy can also move students toward more open ways of thinking and believing. Empathy is treated more fully in chapter 6; here it is enough to say that having students participate in activities designed to get them into the shoes of the "other" for a time will help develop empathy and promote more open beliefs. One such activity is role playing. Clore and Jeffery conducted a study in which a supposedly disabled researcher asked students to spend some time in a wheelchair on campus or go with the person in the chair as an observer. At the end of the experiment, the students who had actively played the role or observed the role player were found to have more favorable views of disabled persons (and of the supposedly disabled experimenter) than the students in the control group, who simply walked around campus.

Role playing that asks people to engage in counterattitudinal behavior can also have an effect on the way they hold their beliefs. There is some evidence from the theory of cognitive dissonance that the most effective way to change someone's attitude is to change their behavior first; the change in attitude follows the change in behavior (see Festinger, *Cognitive*; Buck 428–29; Friedman; Glasser). The classroom debate in which students are asked to argue from the side they disagree with is an example of an activity that invites students to role-play counterattitudinal behavior. In my class, for example, I asked students to read an article about Muslim schoolgirls in France not being allowed to wear scarves to cover their heads, as their religion required. I set up a mock court debate and asked some of the students who seemed to be having the most difficulty understanding the tenets of Islam to play the lawyers arguing the case for freedom of expression of religion for these children.

Of course, we may not see any movement toward a more open stance in our students' thinking processes during the few weeks we have with them in a writing course. Alberto, for example, put a good deal of energy all semester into warding off ideas that threatened his closed belief system. He chose not to listen to the suggestions of his writing group members, who argued with him at some length about his depiction of Islam as "evil." Although he had debate experience, he told me he couldn't take a position that conflicted with his religious beliefs and so did not participate in the class debate on the rights of Muslim schoolgirls. The final draft of his library paper turned out to be another polemic in which he castigated not only believers in Islam but also those who adhere to Judaism (he termed the latter "Christ killers"); his "library" sources were religious tracts from his church. I conferred with him about this paper, telling him that although I would count it as having been completed, I could not grade it as one of the papers he submitted at the end of the semester and shared with him my concern that the portfolio readers would not pass it, since it did not in fact fulfill the assignment. He agreed to submit another paper for the final portfolio readings, and while he accepted my decision not to grade his paper, he was not happy about it. He had simply told the truth; it was a violation of his religious freedom to expect him to do otherwise. After the conference I felt dismayed and worried about him. I wondered if he would ever be able to think and write in a way that understood and acknowledged the stance of the "other." I hoped that if my class didn't have an effect on his closed belief system, the culture of the university and the social interaction with his more tolerant peers would eventually open his mind and heart.

Heather's experience shows how positive, focused social interaction can bring about more open ways of thinking as students develop a sense of audience. Throughout her paper Heather quoted scripture to refute the teachings of Islam. In a conference I asked her how she felt when the speaker quoted the Prophet in answer to questions from the class, and she saw the parallel immediately. We talked about how she could write this so that the speaker from the mosque would accept the representation of Islamic beliefs as fair. Heather's writing group helped her even more. In her draft she had stated that Islam took the ideas of Christianity and "twisted" them. An Mei, ever sensitive to the nuances of English diction, told her she didn't think "twisted" was the right word. The other students tried to help her find another word, finally suggesting "adapted." Heather seemed surprised but responded to this and several other suggestions that helped tone down the polemic. She later told me that it did not occur to her that the writing group wouldn't agree with her, and that rewriting the paper with them as well as the mosque speaker in mind helped her think about how to present her ideas "more clearly." The final version was still more a "my turn" essay than an objective comparison, but there was less polemic and more reliance on research to make her points, a much more open stance.

Jaymie's experience illustrates how an activity designed to build empathy can move students toward more open thinking. Like many other English 101 teachers on my campus, I have one assignment where I ask students to interview an international student about his or her contact with the culture of the United States. The assignment gives students an interview protocol to use, but most students end up chatting with the student they interview long after the last question on the protocol. Jaymie interviewed a young woman in another of her classes, a Muslim from Ethiopia who was a peer advisor in one of the residence halls; like Jaymie, Tarik was very much involved in campus student organizations. Both were intensely interested in the Middle East and spent quite a bit of time discussing the situation of the Falashas, the Ethiopian Jews. Both deplored the actions of the more extreme adherents of their respective faiths. Tarik also told Jaymie that in spite of the fact that she had lived in Italy before coming to the United States, she still had difficulties adjusting to life in our small college town. Jaymie, coming from a city on the west side of the state, sympathized. Her paper on the interview focused on the similarities between the two of them, in spite of their different backgrounds. Jaymie then went back to her paper on Islam and rewrote it, using a similar thesis: while there were many differences, her religion and Islam were more alike than they were different. Her interview with Tarik had helped her see the subject matter from another's point of view. I found the revised version of this paper to be a quantum leap from her earlier draft in its maturity of thought and expression.

Astin's research shows that students involved in activities that promoted diversity and increased cultural awareness reported greater gains in cognitive and affective development, increased satisfaction with most areas of the college experience, and increased commitment to promoting racial understanding (431). Jaymie's growth as a thinker and writer is the sort that makes a teacher's heart leap up. It is rare, at least in my experience, to find such growth in a first-year writing class; most of our students move (as I did myself at that age) more slowly and much less dramatically toward more open belief systems. Some, like Alberto, may never change their way of believing. But I am convinced that this move toward an open system of beliefs and attitudes is one of the most important affective changes that we as writing teachers can help bring about.

❦ 5 ❦

Intuition

> During all those years there was a feeling of direction,
> of going straight toward something concrete. It is, of
> course, very hard to express that feeling in words, but
> it was decidedly the case and clearly to be distin-
> guished from later considerations about the rational
> form of the solution.
>
> —Albert Einstein,
> in Wertheimer's *Productive Thinking*

We are working on the last paper of the semester. After the rigors of the library paper with its precise requirements, I want to give students an assignment where they can satisfy some of their creative urges. We have been reading and discussing selections having to do with how various cultures view nature, as the Self or as the Other: Nobel Peace Prize winner Rigoberta Menchú's "Earth, The Mother of Man," a piece on ecofeminism, another on the Earth First! movement, Wendell Berry's "Think Little," and several on how ancient and modern cultures have conceptualized gardens based on their view of the natural world.

In this part of the country, we are surrounded by natural beauty—and also by controversy about how that beauty should be preserved and maintained. This assignment will, I hope, make students more aware of and help them articulate and analyze their feelings about a particular natural spot.

To this end, I use a guided visualization exercise at the beginning of the class to help them "see" a place first before they try to describe it.

I always worry when I use this exercise—will the students find it too hokey, too New Age? Will they cooperate? Will this exercise, like everything else in the class so far, be "too hard" for Ira? Will Tom and Chad fall asleep? But they do cooperate (Ira is absent, as has been happening with increasing frequency; Tom and Chad snort a little at the beginning but get into the exercise anyway). I ask the class first to sit in a comfortable position, with eyes closed. Then I ask them to relax specific parts of their body, starting with the toes and working on up to the facial muscles, a technique that I tell them can also be used to help them deal with stress.

I then ask them to think about a particular place, a place that is peaceful and beautiful, somewhere they like to be, and visualize themselves in that place. I ask them to look around—what colors do they see? Are some things brighter or duller than others? The place has certain characteristic sounds they enjoy—what are those sounds? Listen carefully—are they loud or soft? High in pitch or low? There are certain fragrances associated with this place—what are they? There are things to touch—what do they feel like? Do they have rough or smooth textures? I ask them to move around in this place, experiencing it from several different vantage points.

After a peaceful minute or two, I tell them to count slowly to three, breathe in deeply, open their eyes, and say silently to themselves, "I feel alert and relaxed." Then I ask them to freewrite, describing this place and why it is meaningful to them. Everyone writes, but Rod writes with particular intensity. His draft, describing a river where he and his father went fly-fishing, becomes the best paper he has written this semester; unlike his experience with earlier papers, this one needed little revision. We discuss the paper and his love of fly-fishing, and I loan him my copy of Maclean's *A River Runs Through It* for his own enjoyment.

He tells me he "knew" how this paper should go right from the start—it just "flowed."

We have all felt it at some point, that feeling of directedness and certainty. In ordinary conversation, we call this feeling by various names: intuition, inspiration, creative thinking, a hunch, an educated guess. Those who write about this phenomenon of nonanalytical thinking often describe it in terms of feeling, hearing, or seeing. Psychologists have referred to it as "thinking with the muscles" (Kempf 23), "knowing with the left hand" (Bruner), "listening with the third ear" (Reik), listening to one's "inner voice," or "subjective knowing" (Belenky, Clinchy, Goldberger, and Tarule). Philosophers, especially those interested in education, write about intuition as "awakening the inner eye" (Noddings and Shore) and as the "felt sense," "the soft underbelly of thought . . . a kind of bodily awareness that . . . can be used as a tool . . . a bodily awareness that . . . encompasses everything you feel and know about a given subject at a given time. . . . It is felt in the body, yet it has meanings" (Gendlin 35, 165). In the field of composition, Perl has applied Gendlin's "felt sense" to writing as a way of describing that feeling of momentum or of inspiration that guides us as we plan, draft, and revise our work ("Understanding Composing"). This chapter examines this affective "felt sense" as part of the thinking process. By understanding the phenomenon more fully, we as teachers can help our students understand how to be more receptive to intuition. We can show them that they need not wait for inspiration to strike but can find ways to make appointments with the muse when they write.

First, let us be clear about definitions. By "intuition" I mean both the knowledge that comes to us without conscious use of rational, analytical means and the process by which such knowledge comes to us (see Harré and Lamb).[1] "Insight" describes a moment of intuitive comprehension, the phenomenon of suddenly "seeing" a solution or understanding structures and relationships. The term was first used in psychology by Gestalt psychologist Wolfgang Köhler (1925) to describe a form of rapid and intelligent problem-solving by chimpanzees, where the chimps behaved as if their perception of the problem (bananas hung out of reach) had undergone sudden restructuring when they saw all the constituent elements of the problem in the same field of view (the bananas, a stick, and boxes that could be stacked and stood upon). Insightful experiences are legendary in the sciences: the "Eureka!" experience Archimedes had in the public bath, the breakthrough that the falling apple brought to Newton's thinking about gravity, the sudden flash of understanding Henri Poincaré experienced (about the relationship between Fuchsian functions and non-Euclidian geometry) when stepping onto a streetcar (Perkins; Poincaré, "Mathematical Creation"; Hadamard). Those of us in the humanities know insight as the "aha" experience we have when we see a new relationship between ideas or sense a new direction for a piece as we write. "Inspiration," a term used most often in the humanities, refers to the affective state of tension, excitement, and engagement felt during an intuitive, insightful experience. The term is often used in ordinary parlance in connection with artistic expression or religious experience, but it is also used in a broader sense to describe the affective state that accompanies all episodes of intuitive, insightful knowing, of being carried along by and totally absorbed in what you are doing—the state athletes refer to when they are "playing in the zone," a state Csikszentmihalyi calls "flow."

Intuition as the Apprehension of Ultimate Truth

The construct of intuition has undergone important changes over time, changes that shed some light on the present understanding of the term. Let us look first at ancient views of the phenomenon.[2] In the beginning, intuition was taken to be not just a way of knowing but to be a particular kind of knowing—the nonrational, direct apprehension of higher truth or of the divine. The ancients, who made no clear distinction between external events and internal impressions (see Noddings and Shore 3), described intuitive knowing in external terms, as visions seen or voices heard: the gods appear to the heroes of the *Iliad*, a still, small voice speaks to Elijah, a light from heaven knocks Saul to the ground on the road to Damascus, a heavenly being appears to Muhammad and commands him to recite.[3] Most ancient societies had seers, prophets, or oracles who could interpret the intuitive experiences of others, predict events, and give advice based on their own messages from the cosmic forces. Eastern religions viewed (and still view) intuition as a valuable source of truth; Hindus and Buddhists achieve insight into the cosmic order of things through the discipline of body and mind in meditation.

The ancient Greeks and Romans, in spite of their emphasis on rationality, also saw intuition as the understanding of and the source of truth. Stories of the lives of the noble Greeks and Romans demonstrated that for many generals and rulers, the words of priests and soothsayers superseded rational conclusions and were ignored at one's peril (as was the warning to beware the Ides of March). The Pythagoreans combined their knowledge of astronomy and mathematics with a belief that numbers (which are intuitively apprehended) are the ultimate elements of the universe—elements that if understood could unlock the secrets of the cosmos. One basis for this belief was Pythagoras's discovery of the precise mathematical basis for harmonious musical intervals. This insight into the relationship between nature and number had for his followers a mystic force, giving him the status of a seer (Bronowski 156–57; the notion of the "music of the spheres"—the heavenly music emitted as the planets turn on crystal spheres in a mathematically harmonious cosmos— is based on the Pythagorean idea that the universe is governed by exact numbers). Plato's doctrine of ideas held that while induction (which operates on the sensory world) can yield conceptions, only intuition (which operates on conceptions) can yield ideas, the ultimate reality beyond the senses.

The mind has inborn impressions of these ideas (or abstract forms), impressions that make all knowledge possible. For Plato, all knowing was remembering, an intuitive recall of the deep structure of reality. In his *Posterior Analytics*, Aristotle referred to intuitive reason, or knowledge of the principles of scientific knowledge, which exist without logical proof. Intuitive truths (we might call them assumptions) are necessary for deductive reasoning, since without them reasoning would consist of an endless chain of proofs. The Neoplatonist Plotinus held that true knowledge is obtained through nonrational "seeing," a mystic experience in which the seer feels united with the object of contemplation. Medieval theologians like St. Augustine and Thomas Aquinas identified this intuitive mystic experience with the contemplation of God and divine revelation.

As Western cultures moved into a more rationalistic, scientific age, the concept of intuition lost much of its original association with the mystical and divine—indeed, since it is not subject to demonstrative reasoning or empirical observation, intuition was often discounted as a way of knowing anything. Nevertheless a few philosophers, reacting against the rationalism of the times, defended intuition as a source of and path to ultimate truth. This truth no longer came externally, however; as Conners notes, the god moved within (73–74), and psychologists began to speak of inner sight and inner voices. Classical intuitionism, as psychologist Malcolm Westcott calls it (*Toward*), held that intuition is a form of immediate knowledge that cannot be understood in rational terms and that is superior to rational understanding.[4] Spinoza argued that intuition was the only route to absolute truth; reason can lead to knowledge of the abstract, but only intuition can lead to knowledge of the essence of the particular—to "knowledge of" rather than "knowledge about." Attainment of intuitive knowledge puts the knower in direct contact with ultimate reality. Reason is not discounted in this process—in fact, the most elaborate intuitive experiences happen in concert with the full exercise of reason—but only intuition can lead to true knowledge and conviction (see Westcott, *Toward* 11–12). Kant claimed that intuition was the source of propositional knowledge, a nonrational recognition of such entities that could not be known through ordinary sense perception. Like Plato, he proposed that the mind held a priori knowings of truth (like the basic axioms of Euclidean geometry); intuition, then, was a way of getting at what was already known innately. At the end of the nineteenth century, Bergson argued that we can use intuition to gain a deeper understanding of reality than intellect alone can give us. This reality (which is dynamic change, flux, movement) is ordinarily hidden from us by the intellect, which imposes immobility and makes possible the conduct of ordinary affairs. Through intuition, we apprehend the dynamic flux of life, the élan vital or life force. Bergson believed that while there is no guarantee that intuition will come when bidden, intuition can be encouraged through the mental effort of freeing oneself from reason and logical thinking.

Intuition as a Way of Knowing and Thinking

With the advent of modern psychology, intuition came to be seen not as a way of knowing the truth or apprehending ultimate reality but simply as a way of knowing (see Noddings and Shore 7). Carl Jung, the first to move intuition out of the realm of metaphysics into psychology, discussed the phenomenon as part of his psychoanalytic theory of personality types. According to Jung, personality and behavior can be understood in terms of four mental functions: intuition (perception by way of the unconscious), sensation (perceptions by way of the senses), thinking (cognition, the forming of logical conclusions), and feeling (subjective evaluation). One's personality is partly shaped by whichever of these functions becomes more fully developed than the others (some researchers have used Jungian personality theory to explain individual differences in writing processes;

see Jensen and DiTiberio). Intuition for Jung is in opposition
to sensing, as thinking is in opposition to feeling; it is the
nonrational, unconscious perception of possibilities, implications, principles, and objects as a whole (at the expense of
details). By "unconscious" he means not only one's individual, personal unconscious but also the collective unconscious—the inborn, inherited understanding of universal,
archetypal human situations (like the situation of Oedipus,
for example). For Jung, intuitive perception of the collective
unconscious leads us to the collective wisdom of our culture
about recurrent human problems. It is a way of immediate
knowing, of connecting with cultural archetypes, but no more
special than other ways, and is modified by the other mental
functions.[5]

In the first part of the twentieth century, psychology
did not devote much attention to intuition. Because they
defined learning as a sequential, step-by-step process, behaviorists did not know what to do with intuition or with
the phenomenon of insight; they defined the latter simply as
"one-step learning" (see Mowrer). The Gestalt field psychologists, as noted earlier, were largely responsible for introducing the concept into the modern psychological conversation.
One such scientist, Max Wertheimer, took the notion of intuition as a crucial part of what he termed "productive thinking." Examining mathematical (usually geometrical)
problem-solving, he theorized that as problem-solvers we
have a need to grasp things as a whole and to see what the
structure of the whole requires for the parts (212). When we
sense a gap, we look for completeness, for inner relations,
structure, function; that search is accompanied by a feeling
of directed tension, which eventually leads to a sudden insight arrived at intuitively rather than logically. For
Wertheimer, intuition involves "seeing" (his descriptions of
the phenomenon are nearly all visual) deep structures, relationships, wholes.[6] Later, Westcott, who thought of intuition
in more limited terms as a special case of inference, picked
up Wertheimer's notion of productive or intuitive thinking

("New Approach"), defining it as an especially high level of problem-solving where the problem is not always explicit or fully defined and the process of reaching a solution is not clearly defined in a set of steps—the solution is in fact reached in "jumps" or "intuitive leaps" ("On the Measurement"). This intuitive leap differs from the inductive leap in that there is less evidence available as to which way one should leap and there are no analytical steps leading up to the leap. It is nonrational and untraceable, where the inductive leap is rational and traceable (*Toward* 40–41). Modern cognitive psychology has continued to take intuition as a form of inference, examining the phenomenon as informed judgment in the context of discovery (Bowers, Regehr, Balthazard, and Parker).

Psychiatrist Eric Berne (inspired by his own intuitive experiences while examining soldiers at an army separation center after World War II) advanced the understanding of intuition by formulating the concept of "clinical intuition," the clinician's quick "take" on or diagnosis of a patient in spite of little concrete evidence.[7] Berne defines such intuition as "knowledge based on experience and acquired through sensory contact with the subject, without the 'intuiter' being able to formulate to himself or others exactly how he came to his conclusions" (4). This is not dissimilar from how experienced teachers do a quick "take" on student papers—in holistic scoring, for example.

Berne's discussion of the process and how to foster it can be applied to other situations that have possibilities for intuitive knowing. First, Berne writes that intuition can and should be actively cultivated, since in his experience intuitive knowing proved remarkably useful and reliable (22); the function can be attained more easily through practice (25). A certain attitude of mind, what he termed the "intuitive mood," is necessary for intuition to come into play. He found that to enter this mood, he needed to establish a "state of alertness and receptiveness," requiring intense concentration (23). Such a state is different from the withdrawn state of meditation in Yoga in that one is able to maintain normal social contact in the intuitive mood, but it resembles meditation in that logical thinking is suspended. This is perhaps why the visualization exercise I used in class and other such techniques (like Moffett's use of meditation) work well for many students. Berne also states that intuition is prelinguistic (as when students say "I know what I mean but I just can't say it")—it can be "felt" or "seen" or "heard," but not yet said; the conscious verbalizations of the intuition are approximations and refinements of the felt sense (26–27).[8] We as teachers can help students verbalize this "felt sense" by teaching them some of the strategies, for example giving them various heuristics for invention (as I tried to do in the visualization exercise—using a heuristic for description involving the five senses).

A Theory of Intuition

If we want students to make good use of their intuitive knowledge, we need to understand not only what intuition is but also how it works. What follows is a theory of intuition in a cognitive psychology framework, based on the observations of those who have written about it and my own interpretations of the phenomenon. We begin with Aristotle, who observed that when acquiring new knowledge, the organism first experiences sense perceptions, then retains them, then at a higher level systematizes them (*Posterior Analytics*). Berne, writing of his own intuitive experiences, agrees with Aristotle's analysis (6). Berne points out that this analysis resembles a cognitive science view of how knowledge is retained and organized in what is now called schema theory—we experience the world, form internal representations (schemas) from that experience, and mentally organize related schemas into networks.

When cognitive scientists write about schemas, however, they define them as knowledge structures that are logical, propositional, and linear—even algorithmic; such schemas include narrative structures (such as patterns for folktales), scripts (such as the pattern of events included in going to a restaurant), and scenes (such as the pattern for furnishing a living room). These schemas are organized logically and accessed in the same way. But there is another kind of schema, one that can help us understand how the intuitive process might work. Mark Johnson proposes that we also form "image schemas," ones that operate not in logical but in analogical or metaphorical fashion. These image schemas are not mental pictures but are abstract and conceptual; they are not limited to visual properties but can have auditory and kinesthetic properties as well. These images, according to cognitive psychologist Allan Paivio, have their own coding and representation system, independent of but partly connected to the representation system for verbal representations: images can evoke or be exchanged for verbal representations, and verbal representations can be exchanged for images (*Imagery, Mental Representations*). This may explain why clustering techniques and other visual approaches to invention work so well for some writing assignments— such approaches tap image schemas.

Many have written about the fact that intuition is subconscious (or if conscious, unaware of its own workings). Berne, for example, wrote that during his own intuitive episodes when diagnosing patients, there was a feeling that "things are being 'automatically' arranged just below the level of consciousness (or, as a cognitive scientist would put it, in long-term memory); 'subconsciously perceived' factors are being sorted out, fall 'automatically' into place and are integrated into the final impression" (26). What is being "arranged" in intuitive knowing? I suggest that when we are working on a particular problem (like writing a paper), we are using short-term memory, mentally reviewing and analyzing various schemas and looking for similarities, based on prior knowledge. But we are also working at another level in long-term memory, working analogically and metaphorically to access "image schemas." A moment of insight occurs when we suddenly "see" the structural similarities between previously unrelated schemas, as when Archimedes connected his own weight to the weight of the crown as he watched water being displaced by his body in the bath.[9] It is not the truth of the insight but the similarities of the schemas that provide us with the feeling of certainty that comes with intuitive knowing—a particular solution "feels" right because the schemas match up so well, like two puzzle pieces that come together with a satisfying snap.

Intuition in the Classroom

This theory of intuition is based on assumptions that differ from what Young terms "Vitalist" assumptions—that is, that creativity is inborn and therefore composing cannot be taught. To the contrary, the present discussion assumes that creative, intuitive thinking can be learned, just as new schemas can be formed and old ones restructured, and that teachers can find ways of fostering intuition in the classroom. In such a discussion, it is important to focus on how psychologists (as opposed to most philosophers) have defined the phenomenon: not as a path to truth but as a way of knowing, different from but not superior to rational comprehension. First of all, such a focus will keep the examination away from such subjects as extrasensory perception, spiritualism, peyote cults, and other manifestations of intuitive truth-seeking suitable for ordinary conversation in California, perhaps, but not for a rigorous academic discussion of the topic. Furthermore, if we think of intuition as a way to truth, we must ask the question, whose truth? Teachers must always be alert to the fact that the classroom is not the place to impose one particular way of truth-seeking on our students any more than it is the place to impose one particular version of truth. If, for example, we use the techniques of meditation advocated by Moffett in "Writing, Inner Speech, and Meditation," we must be clear that we are not asking that students subscribe to the Eastern religions out of which those techniques arose (see Crosswhite's critique of Moffett's suggestions). We want to help our students learn to think for themselves, but it is not our business to tell them what to think.

But perhaps just as important as the issue of teaching versus indoctrination is one indisputable fact: intuition can be wrong. It is, as Berne found in his clinical work, a capacity that is fatigible (25). When we are tired or overworked, our intuition can lead us in the wrong direction. And even when we are fresh, we can be misled by this "felt sense." The literature is full of anecdotes about "aha" experiences of fruitful insight; what does not often get reported is the kind of "aha" experience I had while writing this chapter. My felt sense was that an entire section on Eastern religious traditions and intuition was crucial to the discussion. I was carried along by the similarities between the mystical experience and the more common phenomenon of intuitive knowing. Only when I finished the chapter and went over it with a critical eye could I see that the section on mysticism led in a direction away from rather than toward the main path of the discussion.

But even though intuition, like logical reasoning, can occasionally be wrong, it is still a useful way of knowing, one we can cultivate in the writing classroom. We can do this by first establishing a curriculum that fosters analogical and metaphorical as well as analytical thinking. Noddings and Shore suggest that we need to think about "intuitive arrangement" or "intuitive presentation" of subject matter—that is, one that takes into account the functioning of intuition in the planning of curriculum (116). Instead of beginning a unit with well-defined objectives and asking, "How can we get students to learn these things?," we might begin by asking (as I did on the paper describing a place and its meaning), "What do we want the students to experience intuitively in order to engage them in learning?" We might start a class by piquing the students' interest, seeking to familiarize them with a domain and allowing for rather than pointing out a direction to be taken (for example, if students are reading

"No-Name Woman" from Maxine Hong Kingston's *Woman Warrior*, we might show them pictures of Chinese peasant life or a videotape such as the provocative *Small Happiness* [New Day Films, 1984] that documents the place of women in modern Chinese rural areas). Schumacher and Nash suggest that metaphor and analogy are powerful learning tools, helping students "restructure" their knowledge as well as acquire new knowledge and transfer knowledge from one domain to another. We can make substantial use of metaphor and analogy in the curriculum, for example, asking students to look for similarities among the readings and to think of ways to compare them (in terms of structure, subject matter, audience, and so on). We can ask them to create visual representations of their ideas in clusters or maps, using some of the techniques suggested by Rico. We can ask them to use metaphors and analogies themselves as they write to increase their awareness of the power of such images.

We can also help students understand their own intuitive process as they write. We cannot proceed by having students consciously monitor this process, however. Unlike motivation and emotion, intuition does not accept self-monitoring and assessment; indeed, as Berne notes, if the intuiter tries to analyze or verbalize what is happening, the intuitive process is impaired (23–24). It is a nonrational and nonreflective process, one in which the focus is so intense that there is no possibility of self-observation (26), only of retrospective accounts. We can, however, help students understand the conditions under which intuition occurs and how to establish those conditions for themselves. Wallis's classic work on creative thinking provides a useful framework within which to help students understand the process. Wallis, discussing the work of great thinkers, describes four stages of the creative process: preparation, incubation, illumination, and verification. Preparation involves intense conscious, systematic mental effort, investigating the issue or problem analytically from all directions. Then the problem or issue in question is put aside and not thought about consciously; it incubates beneath the surface, where mental exploration takes place in long-term memory. The moment of illumination or insight often comes dramatically, when one is least expecting it (when sitting in a bath, for example, or stepping on a streetcar). Then verification is necessary, a period of intense analytical work to test the validity of the insight and work it into rational (sometimes verbal) form. Thus rational analysis and intuition complement one another in the thinking process. As Wallis notes, a good deal of creative thinking resembles musical composition (we might substitute "composition in general") more than it does the "problem-solution" scheme described by Poincaré and other creative scientists; nevertheless, Wallis contends, the four stages he describes can generally be distinguished in all fields of inquiry (54). It should also be noted that while Wallis speaks of "stages," he is also quite clear that these stages are not discrete steps but blend into one another and can be recursive; as Perkins points out, it might be better to think of them not as stages but as aspects of the creative thinking process (184–85).

It is clear from the descriptions of Wallis and of others who have researched the process (see, for example, Getzels and Csikszentmihalyi) that creative, intuitive thinking involves intense mental effort. Most teachers concentrate on fostering the analytical thinking efforts that Wallis identifies with preparation and verification. If we want to establish a balanced method of education, however, we need to help students "proceed intuitively when necessary and to analyze when appropriate" (Bruner and Clinchy 83). There are ways of encouraging what Berne terms the "intuitive mood" and Noddings and Shore term the "intuitive mode"—an affective state characterized by involvement of the senses, an attitude of commitment and receptivity, a quest for understanding, and a productive tension between subjective certainty and objective uncertainty (Noddings and Shore 69). Let us consider how writers can encourage this affective state.

Preparation before one sits down to write includes, in

all knowledge domains, a good deal of dogged rational work, especially in accumulating the content knowledge needed for the task at hand. For most academic writing tasks, this work involves such acts as reading, discussion, experimentation, observation, and note-taking. The beginning stage of the actual writing (what Noddings and Shore term the "preintuitive mode") is often characterized by "an agony of avoidance" (94)—almost all writers find reasons not to begin to write. Involvement of the senses in various rituals is a time-honored way for writers to get themselves over this procrastination. Those who are visually minded might doodle for awhile; others might take walks, or take baths, or meditate, or eat. Dr. Samuel Johnson always drank great quantities of tea, sometimes as many as twenty-five cups at one sitting; Amy Lowell and George Sand smoked cigars; Schiller kept rotting apples under the lid of his desk (Ackerman 292–93).[10] Students who think that experienced writers work effortlessly are fascinated to find that in fact they need a deliberate warm-up before inspiration can strike. We can discuss writers' rituals with students, confess our own if we are so moved (mine involves exactly two cups of strong coffee), ask students to think about what helps get them started, and try a few rituals—perhaps visualization techniques, since "seeing" seems to be an important part of intuition—in our classes.

The setting where one works is also important for encouraging the intuitive mood. As Berne noted, once the intuitive mood has been established, the setting often does not matter, since we become "lost" in our work (the literature on creativity is full of anecdotes about "absent-minded" thinkers totally unaware of their surroundings). But most people need a quiet, pleasant place to work, preferably a room of one's own. We can ask students to think about their own surroundings—when and where do they write best, morning or late at night? Listening to music or completely quiet? In the library or at home? (Aside from making students aware of how to establish the intuitive mood, such questions can make us and our students aware that their difficulties with writing may have something to do with the circumstances under which they write. Melanie, the returning student, at first turned in papers that were disjointed and poorly organized. In a conference I discovered that she tried to write after supper while helping her youngest child with his homework. The organization of her papers improved markedly when she got up earlier than her children and wrote in the serenity of the morning.) Establishing routines to help automate the more low-level aspects of the thinking and writing process will also help in the preparation as well as the verification stages. The muse may come unbidden, but it is well documented that structure and routinization will help to invite her in and keep her entertained (Noddings and Shore 98).

Once certain processes become routinized and automatic, our mental capacity is free for more intuitive encounters with the issue at hand. We can help students understand the paradox of making an appointment with the muse by establishing the importance of particular routines for writing in the classroom (for example, a particular time each day or week for journal writing). It is important to note that establishing routines does not mean a return to rote learning. It does mean that there are some matters (like proofreading) that students find difficult and irksome but that can be made through routine use almost automatic (especially with the help of a computer spell-checker), freeing students for productive engagement with ideas.

Students should understand that once they have started to write, their efforts may not immediately bear insightful fruit; we can counsel them to view the resulting frustration as a natural part of the process and to develop an attitude of commitment, receptivity, and engagement. Intuitive knowing is sustained by motivation, by the quest to understand. One way to foster this attitude of commitment is to schedule some time for incubation, for what Murray calls "the essential delay," to mull over their ideas and wait for possible insights, or at least to come back to a draft and see it afresh. The easiest way to do this is, of course, for the teacher to build incubation time into the assignment by requiring several drafts. Student schedules and human nature being what they are, most students—even advanced students who know better—will write their papers at the last minute (see Ronald and Volkmer's illuminating piece on students' accounts of their own writing processes). As Noddings and Shore point out, the teacher can also do much to encourage an attitude of commitment by suspending evaluation (106–08), by establishing learning goals rather than performance goals for students, as discussed in chapter 3. In establishing such goals, our aim is to have students work not just to complete the assignment with a good grade but also to understand the material they are grappling with, to learn something of value. If we succeed, students will be motivated "to try, to risk, to look, to judge, and to stick with the material until it speaks to [them]" (Noddings and Shore 112).

Finally, we can help students understand that they must balance the strong subjective certainty of the intuitive mode with the objective skepticism of the analytical mode. The affective element of intuitive thinking is so powerful that it sweeps questioning aside, carrying us along in its strong flow. Because the intuitive mode operates prelinguistically, however, we must then translate the products of intuition into what Noddings and Shore call "public form"—a poem, a mathematical proof, a piece of prose. We need to work this form out and critique it carefully to see if what we wrote at a fever pitch is worth keeping or if it should be tossed; in Elbow's terms, after we play the believing game we need to play the doubting game ("Ranking"). Again, we need to make this process explicit to students. Those who have had intuitive experiences while writing have a particularly difficult time critiquing what they produced in that mood of certainty and direction. The affective experience is so intense that they become attached to every line of the piece that flowed under their pens (or across their computer screens).

The paper seems right the way it is because of the mood in which it was written. Showing students that we have to revise or even scuttle some of what we ourselves write in an intuitive mode will help them understand the process of shuttling back and forth between believing and doubting, between intuition and rational critique. We can make appointments with the muse, but we also need to make a later appointment with our rational mode of thought to verify that the intuitive song we are singing is actually in tune.

❦ 6 ❦

Endings
Teacher Affect/Teacher Effect

It was the caring much more than the curriculum that
caused me to aspire.
                    —Charlayne Hunter-Gault, "I Remember"

It's the last week in the semester. Cindy, a young woman
from another class, slumps in the chair in my office, clearly
discouraged. She looks woefully at her collection of English
101 papers and then back at me; she is appealing her failing
course grade, and since her end-of-semester portfolio passed
in the final reading session, I have been asked as leader of
my portfolio group to arbitrate between her and the teacher
who failed her. "I know I'm not a good writer, but the teacher
never gave me a chance. She didn't like me." I look over
Cindy's collected work, and while it shows little improvement over the semester, it is not incompetent. I am puzzled.
It is not impossible for a student to fail the class after having
passed the final portfolio readings, since the portfolio is simply a way to establish writing competence, but it usually
occurs when the student in question had not completed other
assignments. I see no evidence of missing work. When I
discuss the case with the teacher, she responds that Cindy's
work is "shallow." I agree that it is fairly superficial but not
that dissimilar to the writing of other students in her class
who had passed. What made this student's work different?
I probe further. Finally, the teacher admits her exasperation

with the young woman. "She's so irritating! She's the epitome of a sorority type—no individuality, no independent ideas; she fills her head every morning with her hair drier. From someone like that, what can you expect?"

What indeed? How much of our students' success or failure is due not to our teaching methods but to our expectations about our students? How do our attitudes and beliefs about our students, our feelings about them or about ourselves, shape their writing and our response to it? Much of what I have said so far in this book focuses on the affective processes of the student writer. Here, however, I would like to focus on teacher affect—that is, how teachers' expectations, their empathy, and their own sense of self-efficacy have an effect on their teaching or on their students. Teacher affect is just one of many variables in our interactions with students, but I hope to make teachers more aware of its importance.[1]

Teacher Expectations: Pygmalion or Golem?

The culture of the process-oriented composition classroom encourages most teachers to expect that all students can learn to write. Many of us have anecdotal evidence that these positive expectations have a good effect on students—that students will rise to the mark we set, especially if we couple high expectations with encouragement and support. The research on teacher expectancies, however, shows that the issue of expectations is rather more complicated than we might think.

While the construct of teacher expectancy originated in learning theory (Tolman), empirical studies of the results of teacher expectancies actually began in research on experimenter bias in psychology. As early as 1927, Bertrand Russell commented that the results of much psychological research involving animal behavior seemed to depend on who was doing the research:

One may say broadly that all the animals that have been carefully observed have behaved so as to confirm the philosophy in which the observer believed before his observations began. Nay, more, they have all displayed the national characteristics of the observer. Animals studied by Americans rush about frantically, with an incredible display of hustle and pep, and at last achieve the desired result by chance. Animals observed by Germans sit still and think, and at last evolve the solution out of their inner consciousness. (29–30)

Robert Rosenthal, a key figure in expectancy research, began a study of experimenter bias by telling half his class in experimental psychology at Harvard that they were working with bright rats and the other half that their rats were rather dull (when all the animals were of ordinary rat intelligence). At the end of the experiment, students were asked to describe their rats' performance and their own attitudes and behaviors toward the animals. The "bright" animals performed better as maze runners; the expectations of the experimenters were fulfilled. Moreover, experimenters who thought they had intelligent rats described their own behavior toward the animals as more pleasant, friendly, and enthusiastic than did the experimenters working with supposedly remedial rats, and they handled their animals more (and more gently) than did the experimenters who expected poor performance (Rosenthal and Fode).

Rosenthal moved from studying rats in a maze to studying students in classrooms after he was contacted by Lenore Jacobson, principal of Oak Elementary School, who knew of his research and was interested in applying it to teacher expectancies (Rosenthal 44). In a now-famous experiment conducted at Jacobson's school in 1964, researchers administered a bogus intelligence test and then chose children at random as their experimental group. They told teachers that the test showed these children to be "late bloomers" who would show surprising gains in intellectual competence during the following eight months. At the end of the school year, those the teachers expected to show significant gains did in fact show such gains; from their descriptions of these children it was clear that teachers found them more appealing, better adjusted, and more intellectually alive and autonomous than the other children. Rosenthal and Jacobson concluded that teacher expectancies for their students, like experimenter expectations for their rats, were in fact self-fulfilling prophecies; they christened the result of these expectancies the "Pygmalion effect" (*Pygmalion in the Classroom*).

Melanie seems to be a case in point. A high school dropout, she had been told by her supervisor at work that she was crazy to think about going to college—she would never make it. At the beginning of the semester she was very anxious about her abilities, mentioning her supervisor's remarks. I looked at her first draft, which was in fact fairly rough and disconnected, but as we talked I found her to be a person of native intelligence and sensibility with a wealth of life experience. I made a point of telling her my "take" on her and repeated my confidence in her abilities as the semester progressed. My confidence in her seemed to build her confidence in herself. Her final paper showed vast improvement over her first; she told me before she turned it in that she felt proud of her final portfolio and also felt that she would, in fact, make it in college.

The notion that they can have such a positive effect in the classroom is enormously appealing to composition teachers who want to help students empower themselves through writing (Elbow refers to Rosenthal's work in his own discussion of teacher expectancies; see *Embracing Contraries* 149, 164). It is comforting to think that by treating all students as if they were smart, they will all become smart. Many of us would like to believe in nurture over nature, in the power of our own ability to motivate students and influence what they learn. But the issue of teacher expectancies is not as clear-cut as the Oak School study suggests; while positive teacher expectations are important, their effect on student achievement is not as strong as first supposed. One study involving borderline college-level engineering students, for example, found that students whose teachers told them they had the potential to blossom did show improvement, but their degree of improvement was still below the class average (Meichenbaum and Smart). Attempts to replicate the results of the original Oak School experiment have been mixed at best (for summaries see Hall and Merkel; Cooper and Good 6–12). The study has been criticized for logical and methodological problems (Mitman and Snow) and especially for the implication that teachers need to treat all students alike; as Hall and Merkel point out, treating students differently according to their individual needs is not necessarily bad (84–85). Perhaps most important, the small mountain of data that expectancy research has accumulated suggests that while teacher expectancies do have an effect on students, the effect is more likely to be negative than positive (Brophy 209). A teacher's low expectations can have what researchers have termed a "golem effect," lowering students' own expectations for themselves (in Jewish legend a golem is a monster, an automaton created by cabalistic rites). As Shaughnessy observes, "However unsound such judgments may be at the outset, they do tend gradually to fulfill themselves, causing students to lag behind their peers a little more each year until the gap that separates the groups begins to seem vast and permanent" (*Errors* 275). The golem effect seems, unfortunately, to be not only more frequent but also more powerful than the Pygmalion effect (Eccles and Wigfield).

Ira is an extreme example. Just after midterm, during a conference in my office about his failing grade, I became increasingly frustrated with his passivity, with what I viewed as an unwillingness to take any responsibility for or interest in his own learning. I lost my temper and told him he needed to grow up. He looked as if I had slapped him and left without a word. I felt terrible. Two days later I got a call from his grandmother (an unusual occurrence, but then Ira is an unusual student). She was worried about him—he was failing all his courses and she was checking in with his teachers. In the course of the conversation I discovered that Ira is the youngest of six children. He was slow to talk as a youngster and has been treated ever since by his parents and siblings as someone who was not very capable. Grandma observed that everyone expected he couldn't manage, so they did things for him—at age 18 he was the only one in the family without a driver's license. He barely got by in high school; she tells me that his teachers said Ira was capable of doing better but was a "low achiever." When the family moved to another state, she suggested that Ira stay with her so that he could learn more independence. Ours was an enlightening but discouraging conversation; clearly Ira had arrived in college expecting that he was not responsible for anything that seemed too difficult. The golem effect had done its damage.

To understand how and why teacher expectations *can* affect student motivation and achievement in the writing classroom, it is useful to look at the phenomenon through the lens of achievement motivation and attribution theory. Attribution theory explains achievement behavior in terms of the perceived causes for outcomes: based on their experience, students develop a set of beliefs about the reasons for their own success or failure. They might attribute an outcome such as a good grade on a paper according to whether or not they thought it was due to internal or external factors ("I'm good at writing" versus "I was just lucky this time"), or according to factors over which they either had some control or had no control ("I worked hard" versus "the teacher must have liked this piece"; see Weiner, *Attributional Theory*). Teachers also form attributions to explain student outcomes. Research suggests that how these attributions are formed depends on three major factors: the student's past performance; the student's characteristics (such as ethnicity, gender, social class, or the fact that he or she belongs to the campus Greek system); and the effect of the teacher being an actor rather than an observer in teacher-student interaction (Peterson and Barger). Teachers look to their students' past performance as indicators of consistent patterns and then attribute success or failure accordingly; thus if a student who has not been doing particularly well suddenly writes a good paper, teachers are more likely to attribute his or her success to luck (or to plagiarism) than to that student's writing ability. Student characteristics also influence teacher attributions. Though the research shows mixed results, some studies suggest that teachers tend to attribute the failure of students from lower socioeconomic groups to outside factors (such as bad luck) while attributing the failure of middle-class students to internal factors (such as lack of ability; see Peterson and Barger 169–70). Finally, the effect of being actors rather than observers in teacher-student interaction—of having some personal investment in that interaction—leads teachers to make attributions that are either ego-enhancing or counter-defensive. Thus some teachers will enhance their own egos by taking credit for student successes and blaming students for their own failures, while other teachers will accept responsibility for student failures and give credit to students for their successes.

When teachers form attributions to explain outcomes, they communicate their opinions to their students through affective as well as cognitive feedback. Cooper found that most teachers create warmer socioemotional climates for students whom they perceive as bright (or as putting forth a good deal of effort), giving these students more opportunities to learn new material, attending to their responses more carefully, persisting longer if they don't at first understand, and giving more positive nonverbal cues (leaning toward students in class or in conferences, nodding, smiling) than in their interactions with students for whom they have low expectations (145). This is perhaps not such a startling finding but one writing teachers need to keep in mind: we tend to like students whom we perceive as bright or who seem to be trying hard, communicating to them our perception that

they can succeed as writers and thereby contributing positively to their own attributions. Conversely, we can also communicate our negative attributions to students, our
perceptions that they are not good writers, and our affective
feedback will have an effect on their own attributions and
their subsequent motivation to write.

Even the most well meaning teachers can be guilty of
misattribution and subsequent low expectations. In their
discussion of remediation as a social construct, Hull, Rose,
Fraser, and Castellano describe June, a committed composition teacher, who attributes the verbal behavior of one of her
students, Maria, to "thinking continuity problems" (310). (To
the observers, Maria seems eager to be involved in discussion and to interact with the teacher, but she does not follow
the "teacher initiates-student replies-teacher evaluates" sequence of verbal interaction that June has established in the
classroom.) Because she perceives Maria as having a thinking deficit, June appears not to value Maria's classroom contributions and undercuts her ideas during discussion; at the
end of the semester, June confides to the researchers that
Maria "drives me crazy" (310). As the researchers point out,
June is not alone in her negative affective response to a student she sees as having some sort of difficulty. There is a
long tradition in American education of treating students
who are perceived as low achievers as if they were lesser not
only in ability but also in character (311–12); these students,
like the supposedly remedial rats in Rosenthal's experiment,
are treated less gently and patiently by teachers. These students become the ones who (like Cindy and Ira) are not wor-
thy of our time and attention, who are not likable, who drive
us crazy.

Students who receive feedback indicating that the
teacher thinks they can't perform academic tasks successfully
will of course become discouraged. Maria, who began as a
self-assured young woman (she had been on her high school
speech team and had told the researchers that she loved
writing), ended the semester by expressing negative self-

assessments of both her speaking and writing ability (317). Some students simply lose interest in learning and tune out, as Mike Rose vividly illustrates in *Lives on the Boundary*. Shunted by mistake into the vocational education (read "low achiever") track in high school, the talented Rose developed

> into a mediocre student and a somnambulant problem solver, and that affected the subjects I did have the wherewithal to handle: I detested Shakespeare; I got bored with history. My attention flitted here and there. I fooled around in class and read my books indifferently—the intellectual equivalent of playing with your food. I did what I had to do to get by, and I did it with half a mind. (27)

Empathy

But there are ways to prevent this golem effect and at the same time encourage the Pygmalion effect in the composition classroom. As in most areas of teaching, perhaps the best way is to understand the phenomenon and to know ourselves well enough to be aware of our own goals for and affective responses to students, to reflect carefully and consistently on our own teaching, and to begin with the affective stance of liking recommended by Elbow: "Liking is perhaps the most important evaluative response for writers to think about. . . . Good teachers see what is only potentially good, they get a kick out of mere possibility—and they encourage it. When I manage to do this, I teach well. . . . It's not improvement that leads to liking, but rather liking that leads to improvement" ("Ranking" 199–201). We can also follow the recommendations researchers make about how to create a warm, supportive classroom atmosphere: deemphasize evaluation and minimize competition, set high but realistic expectations, communicate the conviction that all students can master the material, and express the belief that the material is worth mastering (Eccles and Wigfield 201). We can also cultivate a particular affective state that Rogers has singled out as a central ingredient in the learning process: empathy. "When the teacher has the ability to understand the student's reactions from the inside, has a sensitive awareness of the way the process of education and learning seems *to the student*, then . . . the likelihood of significant learning is increased" (*Freedom* 125). It is empathy that we recognize in some of the best teachers in our discipline, teachers who work not only to understand their students but who also actively try to appreciate their perspective, who try to feel and think along with their students. It was empathy that allowed Mina Shaughnessy to look at the error-filled pages of open-admissions writers and see the logic behind the errors, to understand the "incipient excellence" ("Diving In" 238) as well the difficulties of those we now call—thanks to her—basic writers.[2]

The state of empathic understanding is usually seen not only as an ability to understand the other person's affective world but also to communicate this understanding to the other in a sensitive, caring way (Rogers, "Empathic"; Deutsch and Madle). It differs from the affective state of sympathy in that it does not include pity or approval of the other and also in the fact that where sympathy focuses our attention on our own feelings, empathy focuses attention on the feelings of the other (Katz). To be empathic does not mean to be deeply involved with the personal problems of each student; indeed, teachers need to maintain some distance in order to establish an atmosphere conducive to learning, as well as to survive emotionally (Wehling and Charters 13). But cultivating empathy does mean that teachers actively engage themselves in the thinking and learning processes of their students. When Melanie came up after class the first week to express her anxiety about her writing, I tried to be as empathic as possible. Even though there were distractions (students from the next class were starting to drift into the room), I tried to focus my attention on Melanie as if she were the only person there, repeating back what I heard to make sure I got it right: "I understand that you are anxious. Tell me a little more." After some probing and reflecting back what Melanie was saying, I found that she was worried about being "rusty" after so many years out of school. I told her that I too had gone back to school after having been out for awhile, with some of the same feelings of inadequacy. I tried to empathize: "I've been through it too and I understand just how you feel; I'll try to help." In an interview with a researcher at the beginning of the semester,[3] Melanie was very nervous, hardly speaking above a whisper and expressing anxiety about what she called her "grammatics." In a second interview at the end of the semester, she said that she loved writing, even though she still had a lot to learn, and wanted to take more composition courses; she said the fact that "the teacher really cared" helped her build her confidence in herself as someone who could be a writer.

The research on teacher empathy suggests that there is a robust positive correlation between high teacher empathy and student achievement: at all grade levels, students of high-empathy teachers showed more gains in achievement than those of low-empathy teachers (Goldstein and Michaels 145–50). Students of high-empathy teachers also showed significant gains in nonachievement areas such as self-concept and relationships with peers; the teachers' attitudes and behaviors became models for many students to follow. Moreover, the achievement and nonachievement gains associated with high levels of teacher empathy seem to be cumulative—the more consecutive years that younger students have high-empathy teachers, the greater the benefits.

What is it that empathic teachers do to encourage student achievement? Teachers identified as high-empathic see their role—even with very young children (Kieran)—as that of facilitator rather than authority; they give a good deal of responsibility to the students; and they rely more on collaboration and cooperation than on competition in day-to-day classroom activities. One of the most important ways such teachers behave in classroom and in conference settings is that they respond to students in an active listening mode (as I tried to do in the first exchange with Melanie), focusing their conversational interchange not on what the teacher wants but on what the student has just said. In active listening, sometimes called "Rogerian reflection" (Thomas and Thomas; Teich), one pays careful attention to what the other is saying, reflecting the meaning and attempting to clarify or focus it more clearly. Typical Rogerian openings for class discussions are, "What I hear you saying is that . . . ," and, "It sounds to me like you are trying to argue that . . ." Such interaction not only focuses on the student utterance (or on what the student has written) but also validates and affirms what the student is trying to communicate. It invites real dialogue.

Empathy should not be thought of as a gift, like perfect pitch, possessed by a lucky few and unlearnable by others; one can learn the skill of focusing on and listening intently to another (as it is learned by social workers in on-the-job training). Teachers can be taught active listening skills through modeling, observation, role-playing, and practice (Gordon popularized the technique in *Teacher Effectiveness Training*, a follow-up to his *Parent Effectiveness Training*). Active listening skills are worth learning, because learning the skills that go with empathic teaching can increase the learner's empathy. Teachers who are learning to be active listeners must perforce stop talking and really listen; once they listen and begin to think and feel along with their students, rephrasing their ideas and trying to understand them, they begin to find out that students have something worth saying. Student behavior that seemed evidence of deficiency, like the unconventional readings described by Hull and Rose in their study of students' understanding of text, or like Maria's interruptions in June's class, gradually begins to make sense. As Goldstein and Michaels point out in their discussions of empathy training programs, not everyone benefits equally from such programs—people who don't have much empathy to begin with are likely to gain the least (191–94). Nevertheless, the evidence seems clear that empathy is important to good teaching; as teachers, we should think about how to express and foster our empathic responses. It would seem incumbent on those of us involved in teacher-training and T.A.-training programs to spend some time cultivating active listening skills in staff development programs.

Teachers' Self-Efficacy

Another teacher trait that has been shown to have an effect on student achievement is the teacher's sense of efficacy—that is, teachers' belief that they can have a positive effect on student learning (see Ashton for a summary of this research). This is not just the power of positive thinking; teachers' sense of efficacy will determine the amount of effort they put into their teaching, their task choices, their degree of persistence when confronted with difficulties, their motivation to continue. This is of particular importance in a writing class, one in which it is difficult to measure student outcomes (improvement in writing being the slow, sometimes invisible, process that it is).

The construct of self-efficacy was developed by social learning theorist Albert Bandura to help explain changes in behavior ("Self-Efficacy").[4] Bandura rejected the behaviorist contention that behavior is shaped by its immediate consequences, proposing instead that it was an individual's sense of self-efficacy that determined behavior and that the major source of efficacy information is affect—one's emotional arousal. Bandura made a distinction between outcome expectations and efficacy expectations, since someone could believe that a certain behavior would produce a desired outcome but might not feel capable of performing that behavior. For example, teachers might have a low sense of efficacy because they believe that low-achieving students cannot be helped (outcome expectation), or they might believe that effective teachers can help low achievers but that they themselves lack the ability (Ashton 143).

But it is not only internal, psychological factors that shape one's sense of self-efficacy; Bandura recognized that environmental and social factors also have an influence ("Self System"). In a cogent study of motivation and teacher efficacy, Ashton uses an ecological approach to educational research (proposed by Bronfenbrenner) to analyze these environmental factors. This approach examines the environment in terms of four interrelated systems at successive levels: the microsystem (the teacher's immediate setting, usually the classroom); the mesosystem (the relationships among the teacher's major settings—home, classroom, and school); the exosystem (the forces and structures that influence the teacher's setting, including the mass media and the state and national legislative agencies); and the macrosystem (various cultural beliefs that have an impact on teachers) (145).

Self-efficacy is a situation-specific dynamic; the factors that make up the immediate microsystem are important in constructing the teacher's sense of efficacy. Student characteristics, particularly ability, are among the most important of these factors (Cooper and Good). We all know teachers who feel quite capable of teaching average undergraduates but who quail at the thought of teaching basic writers. Class size is also an important factor (teachers generally feel less effective in large classes), as is the particular activity teachers may be engaged in (some teachers feel more effective in small-group settings, some in whole-class discussions). The teacher's level of expertise in the subject to be taught is of course crucial; many excellent teachers of literature feel lost in the composition classroom. Finally, the teacher's role definitions influence the feeling of efficacy; teachers who define themselves as guardians of standards may face a decline in self-esteem when dealing with basic writing students, while teachers who see themselves as facilitators of learning are less likely to have feelings of self-doubt in the same situation (Ashton 146–49).

Equally important to the teacher's sense of efficacy is the mesosystem—the general climate of the department and the institution, collegial relations, and relations with the administration. Departments and institutions develop their own cultures; the prevailing attitudes of teachers toward students tend to become organizational norms. If most teachers in the department have a low sense of efficacy and tacitly agree that certain groups of students (sometimes even all students) can't learn to write, then newcomers are pressured to accept the same low sense of efficacy and accompanying low expectations (Leacock). I was once in a department where exactly this phenomenon prevailed, a most dispiriting experience.

Collegial interaction is also a contributing factor to the teacher's sense of efficacy. Teachers generally have high social needs but find themselves in a profession that isolates them from their colleagues, often resulting in feelings of loneliness and dissatisfaction (Holland; Jackson). Strong collegial relations can counteract these feelings and contribute to the faculty's sense of efficacy—one of the reasons why attending a professional conference can be so energizing. Studies suggest that enhancing opportunities for collegial interaction can have a positive effect on teacher attitudes and subsequently on student performance (Ashton 151). This is surely one of the reasons for the success of faculty development programs like writing across the curriculum faculty workshops; teachers who are accustomed to seeing one another only in faculty or committee meetings find themselves in a cooperative, collaborative environment and respond accordingly. By increasing the faculty's opportunities for collegiality, such workshops increase teachers' sense of efficacy, enabling them to be more effective in the classroom.

Finally, relations with administrators can affect teachers' feelings of efficacy. Teachers need recognition and support of their efforts from administrators, especially in terms of helpful feedback, but like workers in other settings they also need some share in the decision-making process in order to feel a sense of efficacy (Hornstein et al.).

Outside the institution, the exosystem influences teachers' feelings of efficacy. Legislative or institutional mandates on such matters as writing assessment, for example, can have a profound effect on teachers' feelings of effectiveness, especially if they have no part in determining how assessment is to take place. Those institutions looking to establish gatekeeping devices for students' writing ability should take note. As one researcher (aptly named Wise) warns, a mandated educational policy without involving teachers in the development of that policy (or at least in how the policy will be carried out) will reduce feelings of teacher efficacy. As test scores drop and reports on why students can't read, write, or think appear in the news media, public confidence in education drops, as do teachers' opinions of their own efforts. Budget cuts in institutions of higher education have lowered faculty morale and the accompanying sense of efficacy to new depths.[5]

Perhaps most influential on writing teachers' sense of efficacy are the cultural beliefs that go to make up the macrosystem of American education. Among the most powerful of these are the conceptions of the learner and the teacher and of the role of education (Ashton 153–54). The popular understanding is that writing ability is not something one can improve but is a stable entity—you either have it or you don't. Some educational theorists have argued that such a view of ability allows teachers to explain student failure in terms of lack of ability (B. Bloom; S. Sarason). Such a view allows teachers to learn to live with a low sense of efficacy and accept some student failures as inevitable; if failure is due only to low ability, then teachers do not have to think about the fact that they may not possess the skills or knowledge to help low achievers, or that the system of tracking students according to perceived ability may not be serving the needs of students. The prevailing cultural view of education is that school provides an opportunity for advancement for all those who are willing to take advantage of that opportunity; those who fail, then, are those who are lazy or stupid, or both (Lewis). Teachers sometimes subscribe to this belief, one that not only sustains their own sense of effi-cacy (since students are entirely responsible for their own failure) but also keeps them from challenging the equity of the educational system. Thus, as Ashton points out, teach-ers may become unknowing accomplices in perpetuating the social and economic inequalities of our society (154). Being aware of these issues will help us understand our own reac-tions, our own sense of self-efficacy, and its potential impact on our teaching.

Endings

It is the last day of class. As I pass back the final papers, I look around. What effect has the class had on these stu-dents; what effect have I had as a teacher? Have I been able to accomplish my major goal, helping them think of them-selves as writers? Has the class made a difference? The stu-dents have received their grades; now I mentally grade my teaching as I return their work. Melanie. Her writing has gone from borderline basic to passing; the paper I give back to her is one she is proud of. She tells me that she has learned to enjoy writing but knows she needs more help, so she in-tends to take one writing class each year. An Mei. Her facil-ity with written English has improved, and she mentions that her ESL friends now come to her for help. Rod. His last paper describing his favorite fishing spot meant that he got the grade he needed so badly to keep his scholarship. He comes by my office later and gives me a hug, much to my astonishment, and thanks me for all the help; I find that he would have dropped out of school if he hadn't been able to keep the scholarship. Leontina. After a rocky first paper, she wrote an insightful piece on Malcolm X and his conver-sion to Islam. She tells me that she shared it with her par-ents; it prompted her normally taciturn father to reminisce about the time he once heard Malcolm X speak, a chapter in his life of which she was unaware. Will. He has signed up for a creative writing class next semester and promises to keep in touch. I hope he does. Chad. Halfway through the semester he became much more engaged in the class, producing work that was really fine. He has been meeting outside of class with Ed and Heather in an informal writing group; their steadiness seems to have helped him. Jaymie. She grappled with new ideas in a way that I came to admire. I tell her that I would like to submit her final paper to the departmental literary magazine, and she beams. I feel good about these students.

Then there is Alice. She has told me she is not worried about grades any more now that she knows she has passed the class, but I think to myself that she has not so much passed as just passed through. I wonder if she has really learned anything, if I have taught her anything. I wonder the same about Tom, who slouched through the semester, putting forth the minimum effort. Even though he seems as able as Chad, he just never caught fire. I still worry about Alberto. He has passed the class, but his library paper was so far from fulfilling the assignment that I wonder if he will ever be able to write about ideas with which he disagrees in a way that is acceptable to his teachers. Has this class helped him at all? Ira is not here, has not been here for the last few weeks of the semester; in a final attempt to pass the class he had turned in an obviously plagiarized paper, which according to department policy I turned over to the director of composition. She told him he needed to take the class again. I feel a twinge when I see his empty chair. I always feel that it is my fault when one of my students does not pass. (The director of composition, understanding issues of teacher self-efficacy, later reassures me, saying that she thinks Ira just isn't ready for college. This does not make me feel better.) I have not reached everyone.

As I look around I realize I will miss these students. We spent interesting times together, and I learned with them as I learned about them as writers. They help to build my sense of efficacy as a teacher as I hope I helped build their sense of efficacy as writers. We discussed many ideas during the semester, many strategies and techniques that I hope they will retain; I hope that they will also take with them a positive disposition toward writing and toward themselves as writers. I hope that the affective climate I tried to create in the class will have nurtured that disposition sufficiently so that it will last.

I am always a little depressed on the last day of class, so to cheer myself I read to the students a passage from *A River Runs Through It*, a book they know not only as a movie but also as an evocation of the natural beauty and the ethos of this part of the country.

> Now nearly all those I loved and did not understand when I was young are dead, but I still reach out to them.
> Of course, now I am too old to be much of a fisherman, and now of course I usually fish the big waters alone, although some friends think I shouldn't. Like many fly fishermen in western Montana where the summer days are almost Arctic in length, I often do not start fishing until the cool of the evening. Then in the Arctic half-light of the canyon, all existence fades to a being within my soul and memories and the sound of the Big Blackfoot River and a four-count rhythm and the hope that a fish will rise.
> Eventually, all things merge into one, and a river runs through it. The river was cut by the world's great flood and runs over rocks from the basement of time. On some of the rocks are timeless raindrops. Under the rocks are the words, and some of the words are theirs. (104)

I tell my students that when spring comes and I think of the waters flowing over the rocks, some of the words I carry with me will be theirs. And then we say good-bye.

Notes

❦ Works Cited ❦

Index

Notes

Preface

The composition program at Washington State University has a one-credit writing tutorial attached to the introductory composition course for those students identified on the writing placement examination as needing extra help with their writing. The tutorial, consisting of five students and a tutor (like Susan Parker), meets once a week, during which time students work on the papers for their composition class.

1. Beginnings: Learning the Names

1. These and all other reading assignments mentioned in the book may be found in the second edition of *Writing about the World*, ed. Susan McLeod, John Jarvis, and Shelley Spear, NY: Harcourt, 1994.

2. See Fleckenstein for a slightly different continuum of affective phenomena.

3. Although the categories of research I discuss are somewhat different from theirs, I am indebted to Scherer and Ekman's discussion in their introduction to *Approaches to Emotion* for helping me conceptualize this part of the discussion. A broader classification of past research on affect is George Mandler's; in chapter 2 of *Mind and Body*, he discusses approaches to affect that are "organic" (emphasizing the body) and those that are "mental" (emphasizing the mind). For a discussion of pre-nineteenth- century views of emotion, see Brand, *Psychology* 39–41.

4. The Daly-Miller writing apprehension research is the most familiar application of this strand of research to composition studies (see Daly). For a critique of these differential approaches to the study of affective phenomena, see G. Mandler, "Helplessness" and "Comments."

5. See, for example, the research of Bersoff and Miller, which examines differences in subjects' judgments of moral accountability in two different cultural settings, the United States and India.

6. See Ortony, Clore, and Collins 6–8 for an excellent summary of this research perspective.

2. Emotion

1. I do not wish to ignore the fact that these two theories can imply two different epistemological bases. Such differences should not make it impossible for us to find both theories useful, any more than a knowledge of psychology should make it impossible for us to understand and make use of research in sociology and anthropology. I agree with McCarthy and Fishman's argument that "serious intellectual work requires a full repertoire of epistemological stances" (465). Further, despite their differences, both theories have one important element in common—the notion of construction, both individual and collective.

2. For the discussion of the development of modern psychological approaches, I am indebted to Gardner, chapter 2. The paradigm shifts in the psychological community parallel in some ways the theoretical and methodological shifts in the composition community; around the turn of the century we too were a proto-discipline; those who speculated about the writing process (often professional writers) usually wrote about it introspectively. Later, usually in departments of education, we borrowed the behaviorists' methods for comparison-group studies and analysis of the data generated by such studies. With the advent of cognitive science we turned to a problem-solving notion of the writing process, using the cognitive psychologists' protocol analysis of data and information-processing model of the mind. As we realize what this model leaves out, we too are examining context and affect as well as cognition.

3. It is not that Flower and Hayes were unaware of affective issues; in fact they mention motivation, self-confidence, and intuition in some of their earliest work (Hayes and Flower 12; Flower and Hayes, "Dynamics" 42). Flower discussed writing anxiety and how to cope with pressure in the second edition of her textbook (1985); her latest book, *The Construction of Negotiated Meaning*, includes in the chapter on metacognition a full discussion of affect.

4. In the early discussions of this concept, the preferred plural was "schemata"; here I follow the suggestion of Jean Mandler (*Stories* 2) and the practice of recent discussions in using the Anglicized plural.

5. Not all researchers are enamored of schema theory, however. Critiques of the theory are summarized in Fisk and Lindville.

6. There are, of course, differences in the composing processes according to the task set (see Seltzer; Durst; Marshall; Flower et al.). But interruption is common to all but the most routine and automatic writing tasks.

7. See Bever, who uses the same comparison to describe a theory of aesthetic experience.

8. As Petraglia points out, "social construction" is not a single theory but a rubric under which are gathered a number of theories about social knowledge. Here I have chosen to follow Bruffee's interpretation and application of this rubric ("Response").

9. See, however, Rorty's reaction to this characterization of his work in Gary Olson's interview for the *Journal of Advanced Compositon* and Bruffee's published "Response." See Berger and Luckmann's *Social Construction of Reality* for an earlier discussion of the sociology of knowledge.

10. I am indebted to Kathleen Burrage for this insight.

11. While there are several theorists mentioned in the following discussion, the theory of social construction to which they subscribe is a unified one; see Harré, "Outline."

12. "Inkshedding" is the term for a technique using in-class writing developed by James Reither (St. Thomas University, New Brunswick) and popularized by Susan Wyche-Smith and Connie Hale at the Wyoming Conference on English. It is a method of using in-class writing to gauge and share student response to what is happening in class. It has three characteristics: the writing is done quickly (in five minutes or so) in response to a lecture, discussion, film, etc.; the responses are anonymous unless a student chooses to sign; and the responses are published in some form (usually typed up and passed out the next day for discussion).

3. Motivation and Writing

1. Although it is clear that teachers are most concerned with psychological rather than with physiological motivation, it is im-

portant to remember that the latter is powerful enough to override the former. It is difficult, as we all know, to teach an early morning or late evening class full of tired students.

2. Recently Lepper and Hodell have presented a more cognitive interpretation of effects of reward systems on intrinsic motivation.

3. I am indebted to Dweck and Elliott's excellent review of achievement motivation for my understanding of this strand of research.

4. Task persistence is not always entirely positive, however; as Dweck and Goetz point out (177), it can result in what might be called the "Nixon syndrome"—unusually prolonged persistence designed to forestall admitting failure or facing up to one's limitations.

5. Note that Ira, who exhibits "learned helplessness" behavior in every other respect, attributes all his difficulties to outside factors and takes none of the responsibility himself.

6. Dweck notes that Alfred Binet, the inventor of the IQ test, was clearly an incremental theorist, believing that intelligence (capacity as well as skills) could be enhanced by his training program (Motivation" 103). See Binet 104.

7. Berglas and Jones have called this strategy "self-handicapping." The student uses strategies (like minimal effort or procrastination, as in Ira's case) that reduce the likelihood of success but also serve as a protection against a judgment of low ability.

8. See Stevens et al. for an interesting description of such a project that integrated reading and composition at the elementary level.

4. Beliefs and Attitudes

1. See Anderson's excellent essay on this subject.

2. It is not just right-wing groups that complain about books in the schools, of course; various complaints have also arisen from members of ethnic groups who object to negative stereotypes in fiction—*Huckleberry Finn* is a frequent target because of racist language, for example. But these incidents are scattered and few compared to the organized effort of the political and religious right. See "Censorship."

3. Two of the most populous states, Texas and California, have

a statewide adoption policy for school textbooks. These are states in which conservative groups have exerted considerable pressure to sanitize books in the public schools; if a publisher wants to make a profit on a textbook, that book must pass the "Texas test"—that is, have nothing that could possibly offend conservative constituencies. While the college textbook market is not affected by such pressures, our classes are not immune from attempts at censorship. The growing field of gay and lesbian studies has gotten the attention of the religious right; recently an evangelical minister in Montana succeeded in raising a public outcry over a proposed gay studies class. The teacher was pressured to cancel the class (Gonshak).

4. Kirkpatrick and other psychologists researching this phenomenon distinguish between orthodoxy and fundamentalism; the former involves the complete acceptance of well-defined religious tenets, while the latter involves, along with the belief content, an authoritarian mindset. Hence it is not the beliefs themselves but the authoritarian and dogmatic stance that characterizes fundamentalism of all stripes, right or left.

5. This is the rock on which the "politically correct" issue founders; those who accuse universities of promulgating politically correct ideas do not make the distinction between encouraging students to think for themselves and telling them what they ought to think. This is the problem I have with Hairston's position on diversity and ideology in the composition curriculum, although I suspect that she and I are closer in our actual classroom behavior than our stances might suggest. Her essay assumes that a curriculum that focuses on such issues is necessarily one in which the teacher uses the classroom as a platform from which to teach his or her own belief system and values rather than as a way to move students toward a more open system of beliefs.

5. Intuition

1. I do not include in this definition the phenomenon of precognition (knowing about something before it happens), which is sometimes conflated with intuition, as for example in the work of Bastick and of Goldberg. I also have not included a discussion of intuition as a supposed "left brain" phenomenon, since recent re-

search suggests such a conclusion is simplistic. See Goldberg's chapter "Right Brain, Wrong Theory" and Perkins 256–62.

2. For a more complete history of the development of intuition as a concept in ancient times, see Noddings and Shore, chapter 1. For a complete account of the concept of intuition in philosophy, see Wild.

3. See Jaynes's *Origin of Consciousness in the Breakdown of the Bicameral Mind* for a somewhat different perspective on the external representation of internal events in ancient cultures.

4. For my understanding of the relationships among the philosophies of intuition discussed in this section, I am indebted to both Westcott (*Toward*) and to Noddings and Shore.

5. Jung's theory leads to an interesting question: are there intuitive "types," or can we all learn to be intuitive? Goldberg's answer is that independent, confident, flexible people are those who are more likely to encourage and trust their intuition (109). I would add that because extensive knowledge, experience, and analysis are usually needed before intuitive knowing can take place, most of us are better intuiters in one knowledge domain than in another.

6. Poincaré referred to all intuitive mathematicians as "geometers" because they think visually and take visual evidence as intuitive proof. See *Foundations*.

7. What is known popularly as "women's intuition" is probably the same phenomenon, an ability to form quick judgments of personalities and predict behavior on the basis of scant evidence, without being able to articulate how one made those judgments and predictions. Because most societies socialize women more than men to be sensitive to the nuances of interpersonal situations, such "knowing" has come to be identified with the female. See Rehm and Gadenne 7.

8. The retrospective accounts of many writers confirm Berne's observation that intuition is prelinguistic; see, for example, John Fowles's discussion of how the idea for *The French Lieutenant's Woman* came to him in an image of a woman in Victorian costume, looking out to sea from a harbor wall. Goldberg maintains that some writers (himself included) have intuitions in linguistic form, when the right word or phrase pops spontaneously into mind (74). My sense is that this "mot juste" phenomenon is postintuitive, the linguistic shaping of intuitive knowledge. It does seem, however,

that the form in which intuition comes—visual or auditory—may be domain-specific. Composers of music, for example, often report that they "hear" their ideas; see the musings of Mozart on the subject (Hadamard 16).

9. Fischbein, speaking of intuition in the sciences and mathematics, puts it another way: "In an intuition one generally grasps the universality of a principle, of a relation, of a law—of an invarient—through a particular reality" (50).

10. Even though it sounds eccentric, Schiller's technique was probably useful in more than just a ritualistic sense. Ackerman reports that researchers at Yale University found that in fact such a smell has a powerful elevating effect and can even stave off panic attacks. Other writers' rituals seem more eccentric than Schiller's. Dame Edith Sitwell would lay in a coffin for awhile before beginning her day's writing. D. H. Lawrence, in typical Lawrentian fashion, would climb naked into mulberry trees to stimulate his creative processes. Benjamin Franklin felt he did his best work when he wrote in the nude, perhaps the reason he invented the Franklin stove (see Ackerman; Wyche-Smith, "Magic"). Students may say that they do not have writing rituals involving the senses, but a recent research project found that over 80 percent of college students surveyed at a large research institution eat when they write (Wyche-Smith, personal communication).

6. Endings: Teacher Affect/Teacher Effect

1. Others who have written about student-teacher relationships have approached affective issues through the lens of psychoanalysis (see, for example, the series in *College English* 49.6–7 [1987]). I find the metaphor of teacher as therapist unwise, perhaps in part because I work with new teachers who sometimes mistake the metaphor for the thing itself.

2. Noddings suggests that empathy is a particularly "feminine" characteristic, one associated with the mother rather than the father (*Caring*). There are a number of theorists who assert that collaboration, cooperation, shared leadership, and the integration of cognitive and affective—characteristics of empathic teachers— are feminist modes of teaching (see Schniedewind; Flynn). I do not disagree, but I also find it useful to think of empathy in terms of "connected knowing" versus "separate knowing" as defined by

Belenky, Clinchy, Goldberger, and Tarule. Neither connected knowing nor empathic teaching is exclusively feminist.

3. Here the conflated "I" becomes awkward. Sue Hallet was the teacher of record and Susan McLeod conducted the interview with Melanie.

4. In composition, Bandura's concept of self-efficacy has been applied to student self-evaluation; see McCarthy, Meier, and Rinderer.

5. For a general overview of such concerns, see the Winter 1986 issue of the NEA journal *Thought and Action*, the focus of which is "Affect and Anxiety in the Academy."

Works Cited

Ackerman, Diane. *A Natural History of the Senses*. New York: Random, 1990.

Adams, Maurianne. *Promoting Diversity in College Classrooms: Innovative Responses for the Curriculum, Faculty, and Institutions*. San Francisco: Jossey, 1992.

Allport, Gordon W. "Attitudes." *A Handbook of Social Psychology*. Ed. Carl A. Murchison. Vol. 2. New York: Russell, 1935. 798–884. 2 vols.

———. *The Nature of Prejudice*. Cambridge: Addison, 1954.

Ames, Carole, and Russell Ames. "Competitive Versus Individualistic Goal Structures: The Salience of Past Performance Information for Causal Attributions and Affect." *Journal of Educational Psychology* 73 (1981): 411–18.

Anderson, John. *The Architecture of Cognition*. Cambridge: Harvard UP, 1983.

Aristotle. *Posterior Analytics*. Trans. Jonathan Barnes. New York: Oxford UP, 1994.

Armon-Jones, Claire. "The Thesis of Constructionism." *The Social Construction of the Emotions*. Ed. Rom Harré. Oxford: Blackwell, 1986. 32–56.

Ashton, Patricia. "Motivation and the Teacher's Sense of Efficacy." *Research on Motivation in Education*. Ed. Carole Ames and Russell Ames. Vol. 2. New York: Academic, 1985. 141–71. 3 vols. 1984–89.

Astin, Alexander W. *What Matters in College?* San Francisco: Jossey, 1993.

Averill, James R. *Anger and Aggression: An Essay on Emotion*. New York: Springer, 1982.

———. "A Constructivist View of Emotion." *Theories of Emotion*. New York: Academic, 1980. 305–39. Vol. 1 of *Emotion: Theory, Research, and Experience*. Ed. Robert Plutchik and Henry Kellerman. 2 vols. to date. 1980– .

Bain, Alexander. *The Emotions and the Will*. 3rd ed. London:

Longmans, 1888.

Bandura, Albert. "Self-Efficacy: Toward a Unifying Theory of Behavioral Change." *Psychological Review* 84 (1977): 191–215.

———. "The Self System in Reciprocal Determinism." *American Psychologist* 33 (1978): 344–58.

Bannister, Linda. *Writing Apprehension and Anti-Writing*. Lewiston, NY: Mellen, 1992.

Bar-Tal, Daniel. *Group Belief: A Conception for Analyzing Group Structure, Processes, and Behavior*. New York: Springer, 1990.

Bartholomae, David. "Inventing the University." *When a Writer Can't Write: Studies in Writer's Block and Other Composing-Process Problems*. Ed. Mike Rose. New York: Guilford, 1985. 134–65.

Bartlett, Sir Frederic C. *Remembering: A Study in Experimental and Social Psychology*. Cambridge: Cambridge UP, 1932.

Bastick, Tony. *Intuition: How We Think and Act*. New York: Wiley, 1982.

Belenky, Mary Field, Blythe McVicker Clinchy, Nancy Rule Goldberger, and Jill Mattuck Tarule. *Women's Ways of Knowing: The Development of Self, Voice, and Mind*. New York: Basic, 1986.

Berger, Peter L., and Thomas Luckmann. *The Social Construction of Reality: A Treatise in the Sociology of Knowledge*. New York: Doubleday, 1966.

Berglas, Steven, and Edward E. Jones. "Drug Choice as a Self-Handicapping Strategy in Response to Noncontingent Success." *Journal of Personality and Social Psychology* 36 (1978): 405–17.

Bergson, Henri. *Creative Evolution*. New York: Modern Library, 1944.

Berkenkotter, Carol. "Decisions and Revisions: The Planning Strategies of a Published Writer." *College Composition and Communication* 34 (1983): 156–69.

Berlyne, Daniel J. "Exploration and Curiosity." *Science* 153 (1966): 25–33.

Berne, Eric. *Intuition and Ego States*. New York: Harper, 1977.

Bersoff, David M., and Joan G. Miller. "Culture, Context, and the Development of Moral Accountability Judgments." *Developmental Psychology* 29 (1993): 664–76.

Berthoff, Ann E. "Killer Dichotomies: Reading In/Reading Out." *Farther Along: Transforming Dichotomies in Rhetoric and Com-*

position. Ed. Kate Ronald and Hephzibah Roskelly. Portsmouth: Heinemann-Boynton, 1981. 12–24.

Bever, Thomas G. "The Aesthetic Basis for Cognitive Structures." *The Representation of Knowledge and Belief*. Ed. Myles Brand and Robert M. Harnish. Tucson: U of Arizona P, 1986. 314–56.

Binet, Alfred. *Les idées modernes sur les enfants*. 1909. Paris: Flammarion, 1973.

Bizzell, Patricia. "Cognition, Convention, and Certainty: What We Need to Know about Writing." *Pre/Text* 3 (1982): 213–44.

———. "College Composition: Initiation into the Academic Discourse Community." *Curriculum Inquiry* 12 (1982): 191–207.

———. "The Politics of Teaching Virtue." *ADE Bulletin* 103 (1992): 4–7.

Bloom, Benjamin S. "New Views of the Learner: Implications for Instruction and Curriculum." *Educational Leadership* 35 (1978): 563–76.

Bloom, Benjamin S., and Louis J. Broder. *Problem-Solving Processes of College Students*. Chicago: U of Chicago P, 1950.

Bloom, Lynn. "Anxious Writers in Context: Graduate School and Beyond." *When a Writer Can't Write: Studies in Writer's Block and Other Composing-Process Problems*. Ed. Mike Rose. New York: Guilford, 1985. 119–33.

———. "The Composing Processes of Anxious and Non-Anxious Writers: A Naturalistic Study." Conference on College Composition and Communication. Washington, DC, 13–15 Mar. 1980. ERIC ED 185 559.

Borhek, James T., and Richard F. Curtis. *A Sociology of Belief*. New York: Wiley, 1975.

Bower, Gordon. "Mood and Memory." *American Psychologist* 36 (1981): 129–48.

Bower, Gordon, and Paul R. Cohen. "Emotional Influences in Memory and Thinking: Data and Theory." *Affect and Cognition*. Ed. Margaret Sydnor Clark and Susan T. Fiske. Hillsdale, NJ: Erlbaum, 1982. 291–331.

Bowers, Kenneth S., Glenn Regehr, Claude Balthazard, and Kevin Parker. "Intuition in the Context of Discovery." *Cognitive Psychology* 22 (1990): 72–110.

Brand, Alice Glarden. *The Psychology of Writing: The Affective Experience*. New York: Greenwood, 1989.

———. "Social Cognition, Emotions, and the Psychology of Writing." *Journal of Advanced Composition* 11 (1991): 395–407.

———. "The Why of Cognition: Emotion and the Writing Process." *College Composition and Communication* 38 (1987): 436–43.

Bronfenbrenner, Urie. "The Experimental Ecology of Education." *Educational Researcher* 5 (1976): 5–15.

Bronowski, Jacob. *The Ascent of Man.* New York: Little, 1973.

Brophy, Jere. "Teachers' Expectations, Motives, and Goals for Working with Problem Students." *Research on Motivation in Education.* Ed. Carole Ames and Russell Ames. Vol. 2. New York: Academic, 1985. 175–214. 3 vols. 1984–89.

Brown, Judson, and I. E. Farber. "Emotions Conceptualized as Intervening Variables—With Suggestions Toward a Theory of Frustration." *Psychological Bulletin* 48 (1951): 465–95.

Bruffee, Kenneth A. "Collaborative Learning and the 'Conversation of Mankind.'" *College English* 46 (1984): 635–52.

———. "Response to the *JAC* Interview with Richard Rorty." *Journal of Advanced Composition* 10 (1990): 145–46.

———. "Social Construction, Language, and the Authority of Knowledge: A Bibliographical Essay." *College English* 48 (1986): 773–90.

Bruner, Jerome S. *On Knowing: Essays for the Left Hand.* Cambridge: Harvar d UP, 1962.

Bruner, Jerome S., and Blythe Clinchy. "Towards a Disciplined Intuition." *The Relevance of Education.* Ed. Anita Gil. New York: Norton, 1971. 82–97.

Buck, Ross. *Human Motivation and Emotion.* 2nd ed. New York: Wiley, 1988.

Butler, Robert A. "Exploratory and Related Behavior: A New Trend in Animal Research." *Journal of Individual Psychology* 14 (1958): 111–20.

Calhoun, Cheshire, and Robert C. Solomon. *What Is an Emotion? Classic Readings in Philosophical Psychology.* New York: Oxford, 1984.

Case, Robbie, Sonia Hayward, Marc Lewis, and Paul Hurst. "Toward a Neo-Piagetian Theory of Cognitive and Emotional Development." *Developmental Review* 8 (1988): 1–51.

"Censorship: A Continuing Problem." The Roundtable. *English Journal* 79.5 (1990): 87–89.

Cleary, Linda Miller. "Affect and Cognition in the Writing Processes of Eleventh Graders: A Study of Concentration and Motivation." *Written Communication* 8 (1991): 473–508.

Clore, Gerald L., and K. M. Jeffery. "Emotional Role Playing, Attitude Change, and Attraction Toward a Disabled Person." *Journal of Personality and Social Psychology* 23 (1972): 105–11.

Clore, Gerald L., Andrew Ortony, and Mark A. Foss. "The Psychological Foundations of the Affective Lexicon." *Journal of Personality and Social Psychology* 53 (1987): 751–66.

Colby, Kenneth M. "Simulations of Belief Systems." *Computer Models of Thought and Language.* Ed. Roger C. Schank and Kenneth M. Colby. San Francisco: Freeman, 1973. 251–86.

Conners, Patricia E. "The History of Intuition and Its Role in the Composing Process." *Rhetoric Society Quarterly* 20.1 (1990): 71–78.

Connors, Robert J. "Composition Studies and Science." *College English* 45 (1983): 1–20.

Cooper, Harris M. "Models of Teacher Expectation Communication." *Teacher Expectancies.* Ed. Jerome Dusek. Hillsdale, NJ: Erlbaum, 1985. 135–58.

Cooper, Harris M., and Thomas L. Good. *Pygmalion Grows Up: Studies in the Expectation Communication Process.* New York: Longman, 1983.

Cooper, Marilyn M., and Michael Holzman. "Talking about Protocols." *College Composition and Communication* 34 (1983): 284–93.

Corsini, Raymond J., ed. *Encyclopedia of Psychology.* New York: Wiley, 1984.

Crespo, Eduardo. "A Regional Variation: Emotions in Spain." *The Social Construction of the Emotions.* Ed. Rom Harré. Oxford: Blackwell, 1986. 207–17.

Crosswhite, James. "Comment on James Moffett's 'Writing, Inner Speech, and Meditation.'" *College English* 45 (1983): 400–03.

Csikszentmihalyi, Mihaly. *Beyond Boredom and Anxiety.* San Francisco: Jossey, 1975.

———. *Flow: The Psychology of Optimal Experience.* New York: Harper, 1990.

———. "Literacy and Intrinsic Motivation." *Daedalus* 119.2 (1990): 115–40.

Csikszentmihalyi, Mihaly, and Jeanne Nakamura. "The Dynamics of Intrinsic Motivation: A Study of Adolescents." *Research on Motivation in Education.* Ed. Carole Ames and Russell Ames. Vol. 3. New York: Academic, 1989. 45–71. 3 vols. 1984–89.

Daly, John A. "Writing Apprehension." *When a Writer Can't Write: Studies in Writer's Block and Other Composing-Process Problems.* Ed. Mike Rose. New York: Guilford, 1985. 43–82.

Daly, John A., and Michael Miller. "The Empirical Development of an Instrument of Writing Apprehension." *Research in the Teaching of English* 9 (1975): 242–49.

Darwin, Charles. *Expressions of the Emotions in Man and Animals.* London: John Murray, 1872.

Davidson, Richard J. "Affect, Cognition, and Hemispheric Specialization." *Emotion, Cognition, and Behavior.* Ed. Carroll E. Izard, Jerome Kagen, and Robert Zajonc. New York: Cambridge, 1983. 320–65.

Day, Hy I., Daniel E. Berlyne, and David E. Hunt. *Intrinsic Motivation: A New Direction in Education.* New York: Holt, 1971.

deCharms, Richard. *Enhancing Motivation: Change in the Classroom.* New York: Irvington, 1976.

———. *Personal Causation: The Internal Affective Determinants of Behavior.* New York: Academic, 1968.

Deci, Edward L. "Effects of Externally Mediated Rewards on Intrinsic Motivation." *Journal of Personality and Social Psychology* 18 (1971): 105–15.

———. *Intrinsic Motivation.* New York: Plenum, 1975.

Derry, Sharon J., and Debra A. Murphy. "Designing Systems That Train Learning Ability: From Theory to Practice." *Review of Educational Research* 56 (1986): 1–39.

De Sousa, Ronald. "The Rationality of Emotions." *Explaining Emotions.* Ed. Amelie O. Rorty. Berkeley: U of California P, 1980. 283–97.

Deutsch, Francine, and Ronald A. Madle. "Empathy: Historic and Current Conceptualizations, Measurement, and a Cognitive Theoretical Perspective." *Human Development* 18 (1975): 267–87.

Diener, Carol I., and Carol S. Dweck. "An Analysis of Learned Helplessness: Continuous Changes in Performance, Strategy, and Achievement Cognitions Following Failure." *Journal of Personality and Social Psychology* 36 (1978): 451–62.

———. "An Analysis of Learned Helplessness: II. The Processing

141 ☞ Works Cited

of Success." *Journal of Personality and Social Psychology* 39 (1980): 940–52.

Duffy, Elizabeth. "An Explanation of Emotional Phenomena Without the Use of the Concept of 'Emotion.'" *Journal of General Psychology* 25 (1941): 283–93.

Durst, Russel K. "Cognitive and Linguistic Demands of Analytic Writing." *Research in the Teaching of English* 21 (1987): 347–76.

Dweck, Carol S. "Intrinsic Motivation, Perceived Control, and Self-Evaluation Maintenance: An Achievement Goal Analysis." *Research on Motivation in Education.* Ed. Carole Ames and Russell Ames. Vol. 2. New York: Academic, 1985. 289–305. 3 vols. 1984–89.

———. "Motivation." *Foundations for a Psychology of Education.* Ed. Alan Lesgold and Robert Glaser. Hillsdale, NJ: Erlbaum, 1989. 87–136.

———. "The Role of Expectations and Attributions in the Alleviation of Learned Helplessness." *Journal of Personality and Social Psychology* 31 (1975): 674–85.

Dweck, Carol S., and Janine Bempechat. "Children's Theories of Intelligence: Consequences for Learning." *Learning and Motivation in the Classroom.* Ed. Scott G. Paris, Gary M. Olson, and Harold W. Stevenson. Hillsdale, NJ: Erlbaum, 1983. 239–56.

Dweck, Carol S., and Elaine S. Elliott. "Achievement Motivation." *Handbook of Child Psychology.* Ed. Paul H. Mussen (series) and E. Mavis Hetherington (volume). Vol. 4. New York: Wiley, 1983. 643–91. 4 vols.

Dweck, Carol S., and Therese E. Goetz. "Attributions and Learned Helplessness." *New Directions in Attribution Research.* Ed. John H. Harvey, William J. Ickes, and Robert F. Kidd. Vol. 2. Hillsdale, NJ: Erlbaum, 1978. 158–79. 2 vols. 1976–78.

Eccles, Jacquelynne S., et al. "Expectancies, Values, and Academic Behavior." *Achievement and Achievement Motives: Psychological and Sociological Approaches.* Ed. Janet T. Spence. San Francisco: Freeman, 1983. 76–146.

Eccles, Jacquelynne S., and Allan Wigfield. "Teacher Expectations and Student Motivation." *Teacher Expectancies.* Ed. Jerome Dusek. Hillsdale, NJ: Erlbaum, 1985. 185–226.

Ede, Lisa, and Andrea Lunsford. *Singular Texts/Plural Authors: Perspectives on Collaborative Writing.* Carbondale: Southern Illinois UP, 1990.

Eiser, Richard. *The Expression of Attitude*. New York: Springer-Verlag, 1987.

Ekman, Paul, ed. *Darwin and Facial Expression: A Century of Research in Review*. New York: Academic, 1973.

Elbow, Peter. *Embracing Contraries: Explorations in Learning and Teaching*. New York: Oxford, 1986.

———. "Ranking, Evaluating, and Liking." *College English* 55 (1993): 187–206.

———. "Reflections on Academic Discourse: How It Relates to Freshmen and to Colleagues." *College English* 53 (1991): 135–56.

Elbow, Peter, and Patricia Belanoff. "State University of New York, Stony Brook: Portfolio-Based Evaluation Program." *New Directions in College Writing Programs*. Ed. Paul Connolly and Teresa Vilardi. New York: MLA, 1986. 158–85.

Elliott, Elaine S., and Carole S. Dweck. "Goals: An Approach to Motivation and Achievement." *Journal of Personality and Social Psychology* 54 (1988): 5–12.

Emde, Robert. "Levels of Meaning for Infant Emotions: A Biosocial View." *Approaches to Emotion*. Ed. Klaus R. Scherer and Paul Ekman. Hillsdale, NJ: Erlbaum, 1984. 77–107.

Emig, Janet. "Inquiry Paradigms and Writing." *College Composition and Communication* 33 (1982): 64–75.

———. "Writing as a Mode of Learning." *College Composition and Communication* 28 (1977): 122–28.

English, Horace B., and Ada C. English. *A Comprehensive Dictionary of Psychological and Psychoanalytic Terms*. New York: Longman, 1958.

Faigley, Lester, et al. *Assessing Writers' Knowledge and Processes of Composing*. Norwood, NJ: Ablex, 1985.

Festinger, Leon. *A Theory of Cognitive Dissonance*. Evanston, IL: Row, 1957.

———. "A Theory of Social Comparison Processes." *Human Relations* 7 (1954): 117–40.

Fischbein, Efraim. *Intuition in Science and Mathematics*. Dordrecht, Neth.: D. Reidel, 1987.

Fishbein, Martin, and Icek Ajzen. *Belief, Attitude, Intention, and Behavior*. Reading, MA: Addison, 1975.

Fisk, Susan T., and Patricia W. Lindville. "What Does the Schema

Concept Buy Us?" *Personality and Social Psychology Bulletin* 6 (1980): 543–57.

Fleckenstein, Kristie S. "Defining Affect in Relation to Cognition: A Response to Susan McLeod." *Journal of Advanced Composition* 11 (1991): 447–53.

Flower, Linda. "Cognition, Context, and Theory Building." *College Composition and Communication* 40 (1989): 282–311.

———. *The Construction of Negotiated Meaning: A Social Cognitive Theory of Writing.* Carbondale: Southern Illinois UP, 1994.

———. *Problem-Solving Strategies for Writing.* 3rd ed. San Diego: Harcourt, 1989.

Flower, Linda, et al. *Reading-to-Write: Exploring a Cognitive and Social Process.* New York: Oxford, 1990.

Flower, Linda, and John R. Hayes. "A Cognitive Process Theory of Writing." *College Composition and Communication* 32 (1981): 365–87.

———. "The Dynamics of Composing: Making Plans and Juggling Constraints." *Cognitive Processes in Writing.* Ed. Lee Gregg and Erwin Steinberg. Hillsdale, NJ: Erlbaum, 1980. 31–50.

———. "Plans That Guide the Composing Process." *Writing: The Nature, Development, and Teaching of Written Composition.* Ed. Carl H. Fredericksen and Joseph Dominic. Vol. 2. Hillsdale, NJ: Erlbaum, 1981. 39–58. 2 vols.

Flynn, Elizabeth A. "Composition Studies from a Feminist Perspective." *The Politics of Writing Instruction: Postsecondary.* Ed. Richard Bullock and John Trimbur. Portsmouth, NH: Heinemann-Boynton, 1991. 137–54.

Fowles, John. "Notes on Writing a Novel." *Harper's Magazine* 237 (July 1968): 88–97.

Freud, Sigmund. "Instincts and Their Vicissitudes." 1915. Rpt. in *Collected Papers.* Trans. Joan Riviere. Vol. 4. New York: Basic, 1959. 60–83. 5 vols.

Friedman, Philip H. "The Effects of Modeling, Roleplaying, and Participation on Behavior Change." *Progress in Experimental Personality Research.* Ed. Brendan A. Maher. Vol. 6. New York: Academic, 1972. 42–81. 14 vols. 1964–86.

Gardner, Howard. *The Mind's New Science: A History of the Cognitive Revolution.* New York: Harper, 1985.

Gendlin, Eugene. *Focusing.* New York: Everest, 1978.

Gere, Anne Ruggles. *Writing Groups: History, Theory, and Implications.* Carbondale: Southern Illinois UP, 1987.

Gere, Anne Ruggles, Brian F. Schuessler, and Robert D. Abbott. "Measuring Teachers' Attitudes Toward Writing Instruction." *New Directions in Composition Research.* Ed. Richard Beach and Lillian S. Bridwell. New York: Guilford, 1984. 348–61.

Gere, Anne Ruggles, and Eugene Smith. *Attitudes, Language, and Change.* Urbana, IL: NCTE, 1979.

Getzels, Jacob, and Mihaly Csikszentmihalyi. *The Creative Vision: A Longitudinal Study of Problem Finding in Art.* New York: Wiley, 1976.

Glasser, William. "How to Take Control of Your Life." Lecture. Walla Walla, WA, 21 Feb. 1986.

Goldberg, Philip. *The Intuitive Edge: Understanding and Developing Intuition.* Los Angeles: Tarcher, 1983.

Goldstein, Arnold P., and Gerald Y. Michaels. *Empathy: Development, Training, and Consequences.* Hillsdale, NJ: Erlbaum, 1985.

Gonshak, Henry. "A Furor over Gay and Lesbian Studies." *Chronicle of Higher Education* 21 Sept. 1994: A56.

Gordon, Thomas. *T.E.T.: Teacher Effectiveness Training.* New York: Wyden, 1974.

Goswami, Dixie, and Peter R. Stillman, eds. *Reclaiming the Classroom: Teacher Research as an Agency for Change.* Upper Montclair, NJ: Boynton/Cook, 1987.

Griffiths, A. Phillips, ed. *Knowledge and Beliefs.* London: Oxford UP, 1967.

Hadamard, Jacques. *The Psychology of Invention in the Mathematical Field.* New York: Dover, 1954.

Hairston, Maxine. "Diversity, Ideology, and Teaching Writing." *College Composition and Communication* 43 (1992): 179–93.

Hall, Vernon C., and Stephen P. Merkel. "Teacher Expectancy Effects and Educational Psychology." *Teacher Expectancies.* Ed. Jerome Dusek. Hillsdale, NJ: Erlbaum, 1985. 67–92.

Harlow, Harry F. "Mice, Monkeys, Men, and Motives." *Psychological Review* 60 (1953): 23–32.

Harré, Rom. "An Outline of the Social Constructionist Viewpoint." *The Social Construction of the Emotions.* Ed. Rom Harré. Oxford: Blackwell, 1986. 2–14.

Harré, Rom, and Robert Finlay-Jones. "Emotion Talk Across Times." *The Social Construction of the Emotions.* Ed. Rom Harré.

Oxford: Blackwell, 1986. 220–33.

Harré, Rom, and Roger Lamb, eds. *The Encyclopedic Dictionary of Psychology*. Cambridge: MIT P, 1983.

Hayes, John, and Linda Flower. "Identifying the Organization of Writing Processes." *Cognitive Processes in Writing*. Ed. Lee Gregg and Erwin Steinberg. Hillsdale, NJ: Erlbaum, 1980. 3–30.

Hebb, Donald O. "Drives and the C.N.S. (Conceptual Nervous System)." *Psychology Review* 62 (1955): 243–54.

Heelas, Paul. "Emotion Talk Across Cultures." *The Social Construction of the Emotions*. Ed. Rom Harré. Oxford: Blackwell, 1986. 234–66.

Heidegger, Martin. *Being and Time*. Trans. John Macqarrie and Edward Robinson. New York: Harper, 1962.

Holland, John. *Making Vocational Choices: A Theory of Careers*. Englewood Cliffs, NJ: Prentice, 1973.

Hornstein, Harvey A., et al. "Influence and Satisfaction in Organizations: A Replication." *Sociology of Education* 41 (1968): 380–849.

Hull, Clark L. *Principles of Behavior*. New York: Appleton, 1941.

Hull, Glynda, and Mike Rose. "'This Wooden Shack Place': The Logic of an Unconventional Reading." *College Composition and Communication* 41 (1990): 287–98.

Hull, Glynda, Mike Rose, Kay Losey Fraser, and Marisa Castellano. "Remediation as a Social Construct: Perspectives from an Analysis of Classroom Discourse." *College Composition and Communication* 42 (1991): 299–329.

Izard, Carroll E. *Human Emotions*. New York: Plenum, 1977.

Jackson, Philip W. *Life in Classrooms*. New York: Holt, 1968.

James, William. "What Is an Emotion?" *Mind* 9 (1884): 188–205.

Jaynes, Julian. *The Origin of Consciousness in the Breakdown of the Bicameral Mind*. Boston: Houghton, 1976.

Jensen, George H., and John K. DiTiberio. *Personality and the Teaching of Composition*. Norwood, NJ: Ablex, 1989.

Johnson, Jean E., and Howard Leventhal. "Effects of Accurate Expectations and Behavioral Instructions on Reaction During a Noxious Medical Examination." *Journal of Personality and Social Psychology* 29 (1974): 710–18.

Johnson, Mark. *The Body in the Mind: The Bodily Basis of Reason and Imagination*. Chicago: U of Chicago P, 1987.

Jung, Carl Gustav. *Psychological Types*. Trans. H. Godwin Baynes. New York: Harcourt, 1946.

Kant, Immanuel. *Critique of Pure Reason*. Trans. N. Kemp Smith. 2nd ed. 1787. London: Macmillan, 1963.

Katz, Robert L. *Empathy: Its Nature and Uses*. New York: Free, 1963.

Kempf, Edward J. *The Automatic Functions and the Personality*. New York: Nervous and Mental Disease Publishing, 1921.

Kieran, Shari S. "The Development of a Tentative Model for Analyzing and Describing Empathic Understanding in Teachers of Young Children." Diss. Teachers College, 1979.

Kierkegaard, Søren. *The Concept of Dread*. Trans. Walter Lowrie. Princeton: Princeton UP, 1957.

Kirkpatrick, Lee A. "Fundamentalism, Christian Orthodoxy, and Intrinsic Religious Orientation as Predictors of Discriminatory Attitudes." *Journal for the Scientific Study of Religion* 32 (1993): 256–68.

Kleinginna, Paul R., and Anne M. Kleinginna. "A Categorized List of Emotion Definitions, with Suggestions for a Consensual Definition." *Motivation and Emotion* 5 (1981): 345–79.

———. "A Categorized List of Motivation Definitions, with a Suggestion for a Consensual Definition." *Motivation and Emotion* 5 (1981): 263–91.

Köhler, Wolfgang. *The Mentality of Apes*. New York: Paul, 1925.

Krathwohl, David R., Benjamin S. Bloom, and Bertram B. Masia. *Taxonomy of Educational Objectives: The Affective Domain*. New York: McKay, 1964.

Kuhn, Thomas S. *The Structure of Scientific Revolutions*. Chicago: U of Chicago P, 1970.

Kuiken, Don, ed. *Mood and Memory: Theory, Research, and Applications*. Newbury Park, CA: Sage, 1991.

Langer, Suzanne. *Mind: An Essay on Human Feeling*. 3 vols. Baltimore: Johns Hopkins UP, 1972.

Larson, Reed. "Emotional Scenarios in the Writing Process: An Examination of Young Writers' Affective Experiences." *When a Writer Can't Write: Studies in Writer's Block and Other Composing-Process Problems*. Ed. Mike Rose. New York: Guilford, 1985. 19–42.

Lazarus, Richard. "Thoughts on the Relations Between Emotion and Cognition." *Approaches to Emotion*. Ed. Klaus R. Scherer and Paul Ekman. Hillsdale, NJ: Erlbaum, 1984. 247–57.

147 ☞ Works Cited

147 ☞ Works Cited

Lazarus, Richard, Allen D. Kanner, and Susan Folkman. "Emotions: A Cognitive-Phenomenological Analysis." *Emotion: Theory, Research, and Experience.* Ed. Robert Plutchik and Henry Kellerman. New York: Academic, 1980. 189–217.

Leacock, Eleanor. *Teaching and Learning in City Schools: A Comparative Study.* New York: Basic, 1969.

Lepper, Mark, and David Greene. *The Hidden Costs of Reward: New Perspectives on the Psychology of Human Motivation.* Hillsdale, NJ: Erlbaum, 1978.

Lepper, Mark, and Melinda Hodell. "Intrinsic Motivation in the Classroom." *Research on Motivation in Education.* Ed. Carole Ames and Russell Ames. Vol. 3. New York: Academic, 1989. 73–105. 3 vols. 1984–89.

Levy, Robert. "On the Nature and Function of the Emotions: An Anthropological Perspective." *Social Science Information* 21 (1982): 511–28.

Lewis, Michael. *The Culture of Inequality.* New York: New American Library, 1978.

Maclean, Norman. *"A River Runs Through It" and Other Stories.* Chicago: U of Chicago P, 1976.

Mandler, George. "Comments on Dr. Sarason's Paper." *Anxiety: Current Trends in Theory and Research.* Ed. Charles D. Spielberger. Vol. 2. New York: Academic, 1972. 405–08. 2 vols.

———. "Helplessness: Theory and Research in Anxiety." *Anxiety: Current Trends in Theory and Research.* Ed. Charles D. Spielberger. Vol. 2. New York: Academic, 1972. 359–78. 2 vols.

———. *Mind and Body: Psychology of Emotion and Stress.* New York: Norton, 1984.

Mandler, George, and Seymour B. Sarason. "A Study of Anxiety and Learning." *Journal of Abnormal and Social Psychology* 47 (1952): 166–73.

Mandler, Jean M. *Categorical and Schematic Organization in Memory.* Rep. #76. La Jolla, CA: Center for Human Information Processing, 1978.

———. *Stories, Scripts, and Scenes: Aspects of Schema Theory.* Hillsdale, NJ: Erlbaum, 1984.

Marler, Peter. "Animal Communication: Affect or Cognition?" *Approaches to Emotion.* Ed. Klaus R. Scherer and Paul Ekman.

Hillsdale, NJ: Erlbaum, 1984. 345–65.

Marshall, James D. "The Effects of Writing on Students' Understanding of Literary Texts." *Research in the Teaching of English* 21 (1987): 30–63.

McCarthy, Lucille Parkinson, and Stephen M. Fishman. "Boundary Conversations: Conflicting Ways of Knowing in Philosophy and Interdisciplinary Research." *Research in the Teaching of English* 25 (1991): 419–68.

McCarthy, Patricia, Scott Meier, and Regina Rinderer. "Self-Efficacy and Writing: A Different View of Self-Evaluation." *College Composition and Communication* 36 (1985): 465–71.

McClelland, David C., et al. *The Achievement Motive.* New York: Appleton, 1953.

McLeod, Susan H. "The Affective Domain and the Writing Process: Working Definitions." *Journal of Advanced Composition* 11 (1991): 95–105.

———. "Pygmalion or Golem? Teacher Affect and Efficacy." *College Composition and Communication* 46 (1995): 369–84.

———. "Some Thoughts about Feelings: The Affective Domain and the Writing Process." *College Composition and Communication* 38 (1987): 426–35.

Meade, Jeff. "A War of Words." *Teacher Magazine* Nov.-Dec. 1990: 37–45.

Meichenbaum, Donald H., and Lynda Butler. "Toward a Conceptual Model for the Treatment of Test Anxiety: Implications for Research and Treatment." *Test Anxiety: Theory, Research, and Applications.* Ed. Irwin G. Sarason. Hillsdale, NJ: Erlbaum, 1980. 187–208.

Meichenbaum, Donald H., and Ian Smart. "Use of Direct Expectancy to Modify Academic Performance and Attitudes of College Students." *Journal of Counseling Psychology* 18 (1971): 531–35.

Melville, Herman. *Billy Budd, Sailor (An Inside Narrative).* Ed. Harrison Hayford and Merton M. Sealts, Jr. Chicago: U of Chicago P, 1962.

Minot, Walter S., and Kenneth R. Gamble. "Self-Esteem and Writing Apprehension of Basic Writers: Conflicting Evidence." *Journal of Basic Writing* 10.2 (1991): 116–29.

Mitman, Alexis L., and Richard E. Snow. "Logical and Methodological Problems in Teacher Expectancy Research." *Teacher*

Expectancies. Ed. Jerome Dusek. Hillsdale, NJ: Erlbaum, 1985. 93–131.

Moffett, James. *Storm in the Mountains: A Case Study of Censorship, Conflict, and Consciousness.* Carbondale: Southern Illinois UP, 1988.

———. "Writing, Inner Speech, and Meditation." *College English* 44 (1982): 231–46.

Morris, William N. *Mood: The Frame of Mind.* New York: Springer, 1989.

Morsbach, Helmut, and W. J. Tyler. "A Japanese Emotion: *Amae.*" *The Social Construction of the Emotions.* Ed. Rom Harré. Oxford: Blackwell, 1986. 289–307.

Mowrer, Orval H. *Learning Theory and Behavior.* New York: Wiley, 1960.

Murray, Donald M. "The Essential Delay: When Writer's Block Isn't." *When a Writer Can't Write: Studies in Writer's Block and Other Composing-Process Problems.* Ed. Mike Rose. New York: Guilford, 1985. 219–26.

Nespor, Jan. "The Role of Beliefs in the Practice of Teaching." *Journal of Curriculum Studies* 19 (1987): 317–28.

Nicholls, John. "Conceptions of Ability and Achievement Motivation: A Theory and Its Implications for Education." *Learning and Motivation in the Classroom.* Ed. Scott G. Paris et al. Hillsdale, NJ: Erlbaum, 1983. 211–37.

Noddings, Nel. *Caring: A Feminine Approach to Ethics and Moral Education.* Berkeley: U of California P, 1984.

Noddings, Nel, and Paul J. Shore. *Awakening the Inner Eye: Intuition in Education.* New York: Teachers College P, 1984.

Oliver, Eileen Iscoff. *Crossing the Mainstream: Multicultural Perspectives in Teaching Literature.* Urbana, IL: NCTE, 1994.

Olson, Gary A. "Social Construction and Composition Theory: A Conversation with Richard Rorty." *Journal of Advanced Composition* 9 (1989): 1–9.

Ortony, Andrew, Gerald L. Clore, and Allan Collins. *The Cognitive Structure of Emotions.* New York: Cambridge UP, 1988.

Paivio, Allan. *Imagery and Verbal Processes.* 1971. Hillsdale, NJ: Erlbaum, 1979.

———. *Mental Representations: A Dual Coding Approach.* New York: Oxford UP, 1986.

Palmquist, Michael, and Richard Young. "The Notion of Giftedness and Student Expectations about Writing." *Written Communication* 9 (1992): 137–68.

Paris, Scott G. "Fusing Skill and Will in Children's Learning and Schooling." AERA Convention. New Orleans, Apr. 1988.

Perkins, D. N. *The Mind's Best Work.* Cambridge: Harvard UP, 1981.

Perl, Sondra. "A Look at Basic Writers in the Process of Composing." *Basic Writing: Essays for Teachers, Researchers, and Administrators.* Ed. Lawrence N. Kasden and Daniel R. Hoeber. Urbana, IL: NCTE, 1980. 13–32.

———. "Understanding Composing." *College Composition and Communication* 31 (1980): 363–69.

———. "Unskilled Writers as Composers." *New York University Education Quarterly* 10 (1979): 17–22.

Perry, William G., Jr. *Forms of Intellectual and Ethical Development in the College Years.* New York: Holt, 1968.

Peterson, Penelope L., and Sharon A. Barger. "Attribution Theory and Teacher Expectancy." *Teacher Expectancies.* Ed. Jerome Dusek. Hillsdale, NJ: Erlbaum, 1985. 159–84.

Petraglia, Joseph. "Interrupting the Conversation: The Constructionist Dialogue in Composition." *Journal of Advanced Composition* 11 (1991): 37–55.

Pittman, Thane S., Jolee Emery, and Ann K. Boggiano. "Intrinsic and Extrinsic Motivational Orientations: Reward-Induced Changes in Preference for Complexity." *Journal of Personality and Social Psychology* 42 (1982): 789–97.

Plutchik, Robert. *Emotion: A Psychoevolutionary Synthesis.* New York: Harper, 1980.

Poincaré, Henri. *The Foundations of Science.* Trans. George B. Halsted. New York: Science, 1913.

———. "Mathematical Creation." *The World of Mathematics.* Ed. James R. Newman. New York: Simon, 1956. 2041–50.

Pribram, Karl H. "The New Neurology and the Biology of Emotion: A Structural Approach." *American Psychologist* 22 (1967): 830–38.

Rajecki, D. W. *Attitudes: Themes and Advances.* Sunderland, MA: Sinauer, 1982.

Rehm, Jürgen T., and Volker Gadenne. *Intuitive Predictions and Professional Forecasts.* Oxford: Pergamon, 1990.

Reik, Theodor. *Listening with the Third Ear.* New York: Farrar, 1948.

151 ❦ Works Cited

Rico, Gabriele Lusser. *Writing the Natural Way*. Los Angeles: Tarcher, 1983.

Rogers, Carl R. "Empathic: An Unappreciated Way of Being." *Counseling Psychologist* 5 (1975): 2–10.

———. *Freedom to Learn: A Vision of What Education Might Become.* Columbus, OH: Merrill, 1969.

Rokeach, Milton. *Beliefs, Attitudes, and Values: A Theory of Organization and Change.* San Francisco: Jossey, 1986.

———. *The Open and Closed Mind*. New York: Basic, 1960.

Ronald, Kate, and Jon Volkmer. "Another Competing Theory of Process: The Student's." *Journal of Advanced Composition* 9 (1989): 83–96.

Rorty, Richard. *Philosophy and the Mirror of Nature*. Princeton: Princeton UP, 1979.

Rose, Mike. *Lives on the Boundary*. New York: Basic, 1989.

———. "Remedial Writing Courses: A Critique and a Proposal." *College English* 45 (1983): 109–28.

———. *Writer's Block: The Cognitive Dimension*. Carbondale: Southern Illinois UP, 1984.

Rosenberg, Milton J., and Carl I. Hovland. "Cognitive, Affective, and Behavioral Components of Attitudes." *Attitude Organization and Change: An Analysis of Consistency among Attitude Components.* Ed. Milton J. Rosenberg et al. New Haven: Cambridge UP, 1960. 1–14.

Rosenberg, Vivian. *Reading, Writing, and Thinking: Critical Connections*. New York: Random, 1989.

Rosenthal, Robert. "From Unconscious Experimenter Bias to Teacher Expectancy Effects." *Teacher Expectancies*. Ed. Jerome Dusek. Hillsdale, NJ: Erlbaum, 1985. 37–65.

Rosenthal, Robert, and Kermit L. Fode. "The Effect of Experimenter Bias on the Performance of the Albino Rat." *Behavioral Science* 8 (1963): 183–89.

Rosenthal, Robert, and Lenore Jacobson. *Pygmalion in the Classroom*. New York: Holt, 1968.

Rotter, Julian B. "Generalized Expectancies for Internal Versus External Control of Reinforcement." *Psychological Monographs* 80 (1966): 1–28.

Rubin, Donald L. "Introduction: Four Dimensions of Social Construction in Written Communication." *The Social Construction of Written Communication.* Ed. Bennett A. Rafoth and

Donald L. Rubin. Norwood, NJ: Ablex, 1988. 1–33.

Rubin, Donald L., and Kathryn Greene. "Gender-Typical Style in Written Language." *Research in the Teaching of English* 26 (1992): 7–40.

Rumelhart, David E. "Schemata: The Building Blocks of Cognition." *Theoretical Issues in Reading Comprehension.* Ed. Rand J. Spiro, Bertram C. Bruce, and William F. Brewer. Hillsdale, NJ: Erlbaum, 1980. 33–58.

Rumelhart, David E., and Andrew Ortony. "The Representation of Knowledge in Memory." *Schooling and the Acquisition of Knowledge.* Ed. Richard C. Anderson, Rand J. Spiro, and William E. Montague. Hillsdale, NJ: Erlbaum, 1977. 99–135.

Russell, Bertrand. *Philosophy.* New York: Norton, 1927.

Ryan, Richard M., James Patrick Connell, and Edward L. Deci. "A Motivational Analysis of Self-Determination and Self-Regulation in Education." *Research on Motivation in Education.* Ed. Carole Ames and Russell Ames. Vol. 2. New York: Academic, 1985. 13–51. 3 vols. 1984–89.

Sarason, Irwin G. "Experimental Approaches to Test Anxiety: Attention and the Uses of Information." *Anxiety: Current Trends in Theory and Research.* Ed. Charles D. Spielberger. Vol. 2. New York: Academic, 1972. 381–86. 2 vols.

Sarason, Seymour. *Problems of Change and the Culture of the School.* Rev. ed. New York: Allyn, 1983.

Sarbin, Theodore R. "Emotion and Act: Roles and Rhetoric." *The Social Construction of the Emotions.* Ed. Rom Harré. Oxford: Blackwell, 1986. 83–97.

Sartre, Jean-Paul. *Being and Nothingness.* Trans. Hazel E. Barnes. New York: Philosophical, 1956.

Schachter, Stanley, and Jerome E. Singer. "Cognitive, Social, and Physiological Determinants of Emotional State." *Psychological Review* 69 (1962): 379–99.

Scheffler, Israel. "In Praise of the Cognitive Emotions." *Inquiries: Philosophical Studies of Language, Science, and Learning.* Indianapolis: Hackett, 1986. 347–62.

Scherer, Klaus R. "On the Nature and Function of Emotion: A Component Process Approach." *Approaches to Emotion.* Ed. Klaus R. Scherer and Paul Ekman. Hillsdale, NJ: Erlbaum, 1984. 293–317.

Scherer, Klaus R., and Paul Ekman, eds. *Approaches to Emotion.* Hillsdale, NJ: Erlbaum, 1984.

Schniedewind, Nancy. "Feminist Values: Guidelines for Teaching Methodology in Women's Studies." *Freire for the Classroom: A Sourcebook for Liberatory Teaching.* Ed. Ira Shor. Upper Montclair, NJ: Boynton, 1987. 170–79.

Schoenfeld, Alan H. "Beyond the Purely Cognitive: Belief Systems, Social Cognition, and Metacognition as Driving Forces in Intellectual Performance." *Cognitive Science* 7 (1983): 329–63.

Schumacher, Gary M., and Jane Gradwohl Nash. "Conceptualizing and Measuring Knowledge Change Due to Writing." *Research in the Teaching of English* 25 (1991): 67–96.

Selfe, Cynthia. "An Apprehensive Writer Composes." *When a Writer Can't Write: Studies in Writer's Block and Other Composing-Process Problems.* Ed. Mike Rose. New York: Guilford, 1985. 83–95.

Seligman, Martin E. P., and Steven F. Maier. "Failure to Escape Traumatic Shock." *Journal of Experimental Psychology* 74 (1967): 1–9.

Seltzer, Jack. "Exploring Options in Composing." *College Composition and Communication* 35 (1984): 276–84.

Shapira, Zur. "Expectancy Determinants of Intrinsically Motivated Behavior." *Journal of Personality and Social Psychology* 34 (1976): 1235–44.

Shaughnessy, Mina P. "Diving In: An Introduction to Basic Writing." *College Composition and Communication* 27 (1976): 234–39.

———. *Errors and Expectations: A Guide for the Teacher of Basic Writing.* New York: Oxford, 1977.

Silva, Tony, and John G. Nichols. "College Students as Writing Theorists: Beliefs about the Causes of Success." *Contemporary Educational Psychology* 18 (1993): 281–93.

Simon, Herbert A. "Comments." *Affect and Cognition.* Ed. Margaret Sydnor Clark and Susan T. Fiske. Hillsdale, NJ: Erlbaum, 1982. 333–42.

Skinner, B. F. *Science and Human Behavior.* New York: Macmillan, 1953.

Smith, Michael W. *Reducing Writing Apprehension.* Urbana, IL: NCTE, 1984.

Solomon, Robert C. *The Passions.* New York: Anchor / Doubleday, 1976.

Spear, Karen I. "Psychotherapy and Composition: Effective Teaching Beyond Methodology." *College Composition and Communication* 4 (1978): 372–74.

Spielberger, Charles D. "Conceptual and Methodological Issues in Anxiety Research." *Anxiety: Current Trends in Theory and Research.* Ed. Charles D. Spielberger. Vol. 2. New York: Academic, 1972. 481–93. 2 vols.

Spinoza, Benedict. *The Ethics.* Trans. R. H. Elwes. New York: Dover, 1955.

Stein, Nancy L., and Linda J. Levine. "Thinking about Feelings: The Development and Organization of Emotional Knowledge." *Aptitude, Learning, and Instruction: Conative and Affective Process Analyses.* Ed. Richard E. Snow and Marshall J. Farr. Hillsdale, NJ: Erlbaum, 1987. 165–97.

Stevens, Robert J., et al. "Cooperative Integrated Reading and Composition: Two Field Experiments." *Reading Research Quarterly* 22 (1987): 433–54.

Stotsky, Sandra. "Writing as Moral and Civic Thinking." *College English* 54 (1992): 794–809.

Student Writing Groups: Demonstrating the Process. Videocassette. Dir. Susan Wyche-Smith and Connie Hale. Wordshop Productions, 1988. 33 min.

Teich, Nathaniel, ed. *Rogerian Perspectives: Collaborative Rhetoric for Oral and Written Communication.* Norwood, NJ: Ablex, 1992.

Thomas, Dene, and Gordon Thomas. "The Use of Rogerian Reflection in Small-Group Writing Conferences." *Writing and Response: Theory, Practice, and Research.* Ed. Chris M. Anson. Urbana, IL: NCTE, 1989. 114–26.

Tinberg, Howard. "'An Enlargement of Observation': More on Theory Building in the Composition Classroom." *College Composition and Communication* 42 (1991): 36–44.

Tolman, Edward C. *Purposive Behavior in Animals and Men.* New York: Appleton, 1932.

Tomkins, Sylvan. "The Quest for Primary Motives: Biography and Autobiography of an Idea." *Journal of Personality and Social Psychology* 41 (1981): 306–29.

Trevarthen, Colwyn. "Emotions in Infancy: Regulators of Contact and Relationships with Persons." *Approaches to Emotion.* Ed. Klaus R. Scherer and Paul Ekman. Hillsdale, NJ: Erlbaum, 1984. 129–57.

Verplanck, William S. "A Glossary of Some Terms Used in the Objective Study of Behavior." *Psychological Review* 64 (1957 Supp.): 1–42.

Vygotsky, Lev. *Thought and Language*. Trans. and ed. Alex Kozulin. Cambridge: MIT P, 1986.

Wallis, Graham. *The Art of Thought*. 1926. Abridged ed. London: Watts, 1949.

Wehling, Leslie J., and W. W. Charters, Jr. "Dimensions of Teacher Beliefs about the Teaching Process." *American Educational Research Journal* 6 (1969): 7–30.

Weiner, Bernard. *An Attributional Theory of Motivation and Emotion*. New York: Springer, 1986.

———. *Theories of Motivation: From Mechanism to Cognition*. Chicago: Markham, 1972.

Wertheimer, Max. *Productive Thinking*. New York: Harper, 1959.

Westcott, Malcolm R. "A New Approach to Productive Thinking." Unpublished ms. U of Oxford. Institute of Experimental Psychology, 1955.

———. "On the Measurement of Intuitive Leaps." *Psychological Reports* 9 (1961): 267–74.

———. *Toward a Contemporary Psychology of Intuition: A Historical, Theoretical, and Empirical Inquiry*. New York: Holt, 1968.

White, Robert W. "Motivation Reconsidered: The Concept of Competence." *Psychological Review* 66 (1959): 297–333.

Whitten, Lisa. "Managing Student Reactions to Controversial Issues in the College Classroom." *Transformations: The New Jersey Project Journal* 4 (1993): 30–44.

Whybrow, Peter. "Contributions from Neuroendocrinology." *Approaches to Emotion*. Ed. Klaus R. Scherer and Paul Ekman. Hillsdale, NJ: Erlbaum, 1984. 59–72.

Wild, K. *Intuition*. London: Cambridge UP, 1938.

Wise, Arthur. *Legislated Learning: The Bureaucratization of the American Classroom*. Berkeley: U of California P, 1979.

Wyche-Smith, Susan. "The Magic Circle: Writers and Ritual." Diss. U of Washington, 1989.

———. Personal communication. 1994.

Yerkes, Robert M., and J. D. Dodson. "The Relation of Strength Stimulus to Rapidity of Habit Formation." *Journal of Comparative Neurological Psychology* 18 (1908): 459–82.

Young, Richard E. "Paradigms and Problems: Needed Research in Rhetorical Invention." *Research in Composing*. Ed. Charles Cooper and Lee Odell. Urbana, IL: NCTE, 1978. 29–47.

Index

❦ SUSAN H. MCLEOD is a professor of English and the chair of the Department of English at Washington State University, where she also directs the writing-across-the-curriculum faculty seminars and teaches graduate and undergraduate courses. She has published essays on writing across the curriculum, writing program administration, and affect and writing and has edited or coedited *Strengthening Programs for Writing Across the Curriculum, Writing Across the Curriculum: A Guide to Developing Programs, Women and the Journey,* and a multicultural textbook for composition, *Writing about the World.*